I0030320

The Forex Foundations

Mastering the Basics of Currency Trading

SHERRIE DE KIGUCHI

First published in Great Britain in 2025

Editing, design, typesetting and publishing by UK Book Publishing.
www.ukbookpublishing.com

ISBN: 978-1-917329-63-7

CONTENTS

THE HISTORY OF THE FOREX MARKET

Simply explained, The Foreign Exchange Market (Forex or FX) is an international market for the trading of currency and other financial holdings. This consists of the buying and selling of currencies at a prearranged price, and selling them off later at a profit. The Forex is the largest financial market in the world and its trading activities all take place online. It is a virtual market and traders engage in their activities through technological means. This is done through their computer, laptop, smartphone, or a tablet linked to the internet.

The majority of traders on the Forex include global banks, financial organisations and international companies with global divisions. Trading hubs are offered by certain financial centres where 24-hour trading is offered, Monday to Friday, for various buyers and sellers. Currency trading must be completed in pairs, for example, dollars vs. sterling, with a set base value steering the foreign exchange market. Market forces control trading, which means that the absolute value can vacillate over time.

The foreign currency market is organised into tiers designed to operate with financial organisations and traders more efficiently. Each level has its own vital function, designed for the smooth and efficient operation of the Forex market. Most investors (traders and banks) make up an interbank market behind the scenes. This also includes insurance companies and most other financial organisations as they too have a history of trading over the past decade

Also, this foreign exchange market promotes global trading through currency conversion, which provides easier and discounted business transactions. An example of this is where Forex trading has enabled the import and export of goods and services, by countries, regions or even continents, in the form of trading units.

The history of the Forex market can best be explained through the relating of a series of events, and the methods and systems that have shaped it.

The Gold Standard System

The Gold System, established in 1875, proved to be a pivotal moment in the history of the foreign exchange market. Previously, gold and silver were used as methods of payment in trade, but their values fluctuated, depending on supply and demand. Certain events, such as the discovery of a new gold mine, for example, caused the price of gold to drop as the available quantities of it increased.

The Gold Standard was established by governments to provide security to the conversion rates of currency into gold and vice versa. A specific price per quantity was decided, which established stability among conversion rates. Currencies were now guaranteed by a particular quantity of gold, which in turn ensured that conversion rates were not now tied to the demand and supply of gold. Governments were now required to maintain a supply of gold to meet exchange obligations and this in turn created greater overall financial stability.

The exchange rate trading process became established during the late nineteenth century when all of the countries participating in trade agreed a standard price for an ounce of gold. However, due to time lags, differences in this standard price formed the foundation for the exchange rate between currencies. This resulted in the initial standard exchange rate between two currencies, a system that is still used to trade today.

World War I caused a collapse in the gold standard agreement due to the conflict between Germany and the other European countries. Financing military equipment became urgent, and countries printed money to achieve this.

The requirements were so extensive, however, that the store of gold held by each country was insufficient to exchange for the additional money printed.

The gold standard attempted to recover during the war years but was almost completely out of use by the Second World War. Despite this, it is still used as the ultimate source of monetary worth.

Bretton Woods System

Prior to the outbreak of World War II, the Allied Nations established a monetary system to fill the void created by the downfall of the gold standard system. Seven hundred delegates from the Allied Nations met in 1944 in Bretton Woods, New Hampshire, USA, to discuss the creation of a new standardised monetary system. This would come to be known as the Bretton Woods System.

Arising from this meeting came the following:

- A structure for fixed exchange rates;
- Recognition of the dollar as the most secure currency, replacing the gold standard system;
- The establishment of several global organisations for the purpose of administering economic activities worldwide. These included the International Monetary Fund (IMF) and the General Agreement on Trade and Tariffs (GATT).

The Bretton Woods Summit was mainly characterised by the decision made to substitute the gold standard system with the US Dollar as the main method for converting the world's currencies. In addition to this, the US dollar was the only currency entitled to be backed by gold. This, however, turned out to be one of the main reasons for its downfall as a system over the next 25 years. Gold reserves were so depleted by the early 1970s that there simply wasn't enough gold to back all of the printed dollars held by the global banks in their reserves.

In 1971, President Richard Nixon closed the window on the gold standards system, a major setback to the Bretton Woods strategies and when the US halted the exchange of American dollars for gold this, in effect, ended the Bretton Woods system. Although ended, Bretton Woods left an indelible mark on today's financial markets as it gave rise to the establishment of several institutions in the 1940s, which in turn laid the foundations for the World Trade Organization.

Basics of the Forex Market

The Forex leads the world's financial markets, with participants both large and small. Its daily turnover has been estimated at $1 trillion, a figure greater than the combined activities of all of the other US equity markets combined. The name, foreign exchange, comes from the type of trading it is involved with: the concurrent buying and selling of several currencies at a profit. It must be noted that currencies have to be traded in pairs, e.g. EUR and USD.

Only 5% of the daily turnover of the Forex market consists of governments and companies trading products and services abroad. A much higher percentage of the daily trades and returns consists of international companies transferring their foreign profits into their local currency.

The bulk of the trading revenues are made through speculation banking, which is where banks, financial organisations and traders purchase a specific currency and hold on to it until they can sell it for a profit. An example would be buying American dollars and gambling that they will increase in value against the Yen.

Experienced traders know how to make a profit from forecasting patterns in a certain currency through reading specific market pointers like the current economic circumstances and the status of the political environment. The 24-hour market opens in Sydney and sweeps across the world as each day begins in the financial centres. This allows traders to respond quickly to any market variations caused by several market indicators as they happen. As a result, the market is extremely tenuous and fast paced, with investors in Forex poised to make the vital financial decision: to buy or to sell.

The Foreign Exchange Market can also be called Over the Counter (OTC) because traders also carry out business deals between themselves by electronic methods.

Forex Market Dynamics

To the uninitiated, the first glance at a foreign exchange quote will appear confusing, but an explanation on the workings of the market will provide the knowledge to decode the quotes and interpret the information provided on the Forex market. The most basic information is the first currency displayed is the base currency and that the value of this is set as 1.

The US dollar is most commonly set as the base currency in the markets for financial quotes. It is usually paired as follows: USD/JPY and USD/CAD. The quotes are usually stated as a unit of $1 USD of the other currency listed in the pair.

There are three exemptions to this: the British pound (GBP); the Australian dollar (AUD); and the Euro (EUR). With these it is common to see the pair recorded as GBP/USD, which means that the base value is the base rate and an increase in value describes a weak dollar and vice versa. If the base value gains value this means that the dollar has increased in value and its pair currency has lost its strength against the dollar. The trader can then obtain profit by selling dollars against the other currency. On the other hand, if the base value depreciates, the other currency in the pair is described as having 'obtained' and can then be sold for dollars.

Due to the volatile nature of the Forex market, the value of currencies can fluctuate over a short period. Therefore, traders in the market constantly watch and observe it for every possible opening. An example of this was when Bruit was launched in the news, it led to dramatic currency fluctuations exploited by traders to make a huge profit. Traders need to be in tune with current affairs worldwide to be able to predict with some accuracy the currencies to trade against. Advancements in technology have progressed this process as search robots are commonly used by most financial organisations to track and monitor the market and to make informed decisions whether to buy or sell, with no need for human intervention.

Two-faced quotes are used for trading with foreign currencies and these are made up of a bid and an offer. The bid is the price for the sale of the base currency and the offer is the price to buy it. This technical jargon is used by traders to cut down on long-winded conversations when short comments are all that are necessary.

Forex Market Size and Growth

Of all the global markets the Forex demonstrates the greatest level of unpredictability. Although dealers (banks and financial organisations) and governments are major market traders, the technology and legislation prefer and support individual trading. In 2010, the Triennial Central Bank quoted that the daily turnover reached $3.98 trillion, with $1.5 trillion supplied by spot transactions and the remaining $2.5 trillion traded outright.

Information released during this time also quoted the UK as the leading provider of exchanges, having provided 36.7% of the overall Forex market exchanges. In comparison, the US provided 17.9% and Japan only provided 6.2%. In 2013, the UK increased its volume to 41%, but this figure reduced during the past three years back to 37%. Most countries trading in the Forex markets permit the trade of derivative products, which has promoted the expansion of the markets over the years.

The name, Forex markets, is more commonly accepted than 'foreign exchange markets' due to the sanctioning of the trading in derivatives, and the majority of the developed countries active in forex trade have convertible capital accounts. However, there are certain governments that do not permit the trade of derivatives because of their capital controls. Emerging economies such as South Africa and India favour trading in derivatives and have created currency exchanges for the future despite their capital controls.

The increase in trading in Forex during the past 20 years can be traced to an overall intensification in trading activity and the strengthening of foreign exchange being treated as an asset. This intensification can be trailed back to the progress made in electronic trading as it has allowed traders to improve and increase their buying and selling activities of derivatives and other assets. Retail investors have also played their part as now sole traders can trade easily on their own personal technological devices.

Transaction costs have been greatly reduced, mainly through the development of electronic execution systems and multiple methods and devices on which to trade. This has increased the market liquidity. These have made it more attractive for a greater number of customers to participate. Electronic trading has become so accessible that there are individuals who are earning their main source of income trading in Forex, which has continued to expand and swell its liquidity.

Due to this ease of access, traders and investors can negotiate directly in the market, without the need for intermediaries, and can immediately benefit from market changes themselves. London is the largest global centre for the foreign exchange market in the world and so, when the IMF generates their drawings, at noon they use London market prices.

Market Players

The Forex market is organised into tiers or layers and each investor or trader has their own level of access. This is different to a stock exchange, where all participants enter at the same single point of access.

The highest level is operated by the interbank exchange market where the larger traders, such as commercial banks and security dealers, operate. Down from this resides the traders who fill the gaps between bids and ask prices for several different types of assets traded in the Forex. The variances between the ask prices increase the further down the tiers with the maximum level found between the lowest entry level and the highest.

These variances can be explained by the volume of trade carried out by the traders. Those who can carry out transactions of tremendous volume can demand a greater decrease in disparity between the asking price and the bid price. This is known as a better spread and has a similar principle to economies of scale. The levels or tiers of access are generated and governed by the volume of money traded by the investors. At the highest level, the interbank exchange market, 51% of the overall transactions take place.

The remainder of the market consists of smaller financial organisations, securities dealers, multinational-companies and retail market traders. Since 2004, the Forex market has also seen constant growth, fuelled by insurance companies and mutual and pension funds.

Central banks also participate by trading to keep their currencies in line with the current economic conditions and not experience dramatic depreciations or inflation.

Corporate Organisations

A large percentage of the Forex market is made up of extremely large companies buying and selling goods and services through multiple currencies. Compared to banks, smaller commercial enterprises only trade small amounts of money but, all together, they make up a majority stake in the level of trade. They have a more short-term influence on the market, but the corporate organisations make up the greater volume of reliable, long-term trade, which is necessary for a viable outlook for Forex trade and deciding the direction of currency exchange rates.

Central Banks

Each country has a central bank whose function it is to make use of foreign currency trading to ensure a stable regional currency. Another function is to ensure supervision over interest rates and money supply and inflation. Central banks are also responsible for protecting their countries from economic situations by setting official and unofficial rates for currencies and using their foreign exchange reserves to maintain balance. An example of this would be when imports exceed exports, foreign currency reserves are discharged to prevent a shortfall in foreign currencies. Central banks are also instrumental in controlling speculation traders who profit from extreme market conditions.

Therefore, central banks do not concentrate on making a profit, but rather protecting their country from extreme market conditions that might increase inflation and lose control of the money supply.

Foreign Trade Fixing

Foreign exchange fixing denotes when the central bank of each country sets the exchange rate for that country. Fixing is carried out so that the performance of their currency can be compared to the set base currency, which is usually the US dollar.

Ideally, fixing rates reflect the actual value of the market stability and are used by banks and traders to indicate the state of the market and so to maintain its balance.

Reports or the prospect of an intercession in the foreign exchange market by the central bank can be sufficient to stabilise (or destabilise) a currency in a region, which can lead to stability in trading. If a country has a 'dirty float money system' then more forceful involvement can take place multiple times during the year. Intercession is not always successful, however, and the economic climate may deter the central banks in achieving their goal or failing in their tactics.

Should this occur, a country will encounter inflation and free money supply, which would lead to the value of its currency falling below the expected levels.

Investment Firms

Investment management companies maintain huge amounts of funds for their members and decide on what best to invest this money for them. Examples of these funds include pension funds and endowment policies. They use the Forex market to enable them to trade in foreign securities.

For example, an international portfolio manager needs to carefully formulate a plan to buy and sell multiple pairs of foreign currencies to satisfy their foreign security sales requirements. Several investment administration organisations speculate in exchange dealings in order to increase their profits.

Retail Foreign Currency Traders

Recently, speculating sole traders have made up a large percentage of the Forex market, especially following the inclusion of retail foreign exchange trading. Currently, Forex retail traders partake in indirect trading with the help of banks and brokers to make profits. In America, due to the rise in foreign exchange fraud, retail traders have come under greater control by the relevant authorities, and now these federal regulations require all retail traders who wish to trademust be registered with the Commodity Futures Trading Commission (CFTC) and the National Futures Association (NFA). This registration ensures that traders are protected and that the trading environment is safe. The FCA the financial conduct autothority would be the English counterpart to this though no registration is required in the United Kingdom additionally forex trading in the United Kingdom is tax free as it is considered gambling.

There are two conventional types of Forex brokers who provide speculative currency trading opportunities: the market makers; and brokers. Market dealers have a main role to play as they act as the main players in trades and can determine the prices they are ready to trade. Brokers, however, have a wider function as their role is to negotiate optimum prices in the market for retail orders and they trade for their clients in retail foreign exchange trades.

Non-Bank Foreign Exchange Companies

Non-bank exchange companies are organisations that enable the transfer of international payments to organisations and sole traders. They are also known as foreign exchange brokers because, although they are vital central players, they do not participate in trading: only payments. They arrange direct currency payments to bank accounts and calculate any currency conversions this may include.

Foreign exchange companies make up 14% of all of the currency payments in the UK, and earn revenue through offering better exchange rates than the banks to their clients. These exchange companies are identifiable from money remittance and transfer companies by the greater volume of the services they deal with. For example, one such Indian company provides transaction volumes of over $2 billion USD per day.

Due to their smaller size, these companies do not compete strongly with developed foreign currency market companies. Despite this, the number of online foreign businesses entering the foreign exchange market is increasing, which has provided other options for methods of payment.

Money Remittance and Transfer Companies

Money remittance and transfer companies are some of the main participants in the Forex market, in particular, in Africa and Asia, which is where the majority of their transactions occur. These companies place no threshold on their volume of operations, no deal is too high or too low. Immigrants to the UK and the US use their companies to transfer money back to their countries of origin without incurring large transaction fees. In 2007, $370 billion was transferred in this way, but over the last decade this figure has increased dramatically to almost one trillion US dollars transferred each year.

The world leading markets for money remittance and transfer are China, India, the Philippines, Africa and Mexico. In order, the largest market is the Western Union with over 300k agents globally, UAE is second and the Bureau de Change is in third place. The agents for these are most commonly found in locations such as airports and tourist locations, to assist with the smooth exchange of money from one currency to another. This ease of access and rates that are cheaper than commercial banks explains their popularity and increase of use.

Money Remittance and Transfer Companies

DEFINITIONS & TERMINOLOGY

What is a Currency Pair?

A currency pair is a pricing structure that consists of quotations of various currencies trading in the financial markets. One currency's value is decided by comparing it to the value of another currency, which is why 'pairs' are necessary. The base currency is the first one to appear on a currency pair and the second is known as the quote currency. Simply, a currency pair refers to the cost of one unit of the base currency.

Major Currency Pairs

There are as many currencies as there are in the world that are trading in the Forex markets. This figure fluctuates, however, because the actual number of currencies changes as they enter and leave the Forex markets. The classification of currency pairs occurs through the quantities traded in the market daily.

The major world currencies are those that normally carry out the majority of their trades with the US dollar. These currency pairs are EUR/USD, USD/JPY, USD/CAD, AUD/USD, and USD/CHF. Despite this, these currencies are not considered stable as they trade for 34-hours a day and have very narrow spreads.

What is the lot size in Forex?

The standard lot is a quantity that tallies to 100,000 units of the base currency in the Forex markets. In other words, a standard lot is the counterpart to the trade size. The three agreed lot sizes are: a standard lot; a mini-lot; and a micro-lot.

What is a unit in Forex?

When one micro of the EUR/USD is traded, a pip is worth $0.1, as opposed to $10 on an ordinary lot. It is normal to compare one mini lot to 10,000 units of the base currency.

What do lots mean in stocks?

In terms of stocks, a lot is the quantity of shares purchased in a single transaction. In terms of the possibilities available, a lot refers to the number of contracts comprising a single derivative security. Therefore, the notion of lots allows the financial markets to standardise price quotes.

What is candle trading?

A (Japanese) candlestick chart is a financial chart used to demonstrate the price movements in multiple security derivatives or currencies. Each candlestick shows the daily price movements and the candlestick of one month will illustrate the 20 trading days that correlate with the 20 business days of that month.

The main part of the candlestick usually symbolises the variance in open and close rates for a specified reporting period. The larger the body, the more volatile the interlude between the open and close rate, and vice versa. The colour of the body also provides details for analysis. A hollow candlestick at the bottom denotes the initial rate, while the lower section denotes the closing price. Alternatively, a filled candlestick indicates that the opening rate is at the bottom and the closing rate is found at the top.

Point in percentage (PIP)

In the Forex market a pip is the point at which profits and losses are calculated. When trading a mini lot, a pip is approximately worth one unit of the currency in which the account transaction is controlled. It can calculate the extent of change in the exchange rates of a currency pair. When currency pairs are stated to four decimal places, a pip is equivalent to 0.0001. However, Yen based currency pairs are an exception: they are stated to two decimal places.

How much is a PIP in Forex trading?

To understand a pip in the context of Forex trading, a case scenario where a quote of between 1.1200 to 1.1205 will be assumed. In this example there would be a change of five pips. Therefore, to calculate the value of one pip in a currency pair, divide one pip to decimal form (0.0001) by the prevailing currency rate and multiply it by the approximate volume of trade.

Spread

To understand spread, it is first necessary to know that currency market prices are stated as currency market pairs or the exchange rate quotation (where the proportional value of one currency is shown in the units of another currency). A bid is when an exchange rate is used for a customer trying to complete a purchase: it is the highest price paid for a currency pair. A price quote currency selling is known as an 'ask': this is the lowest price a currency pair can be offered for sale.

The difference between the ask price and bid price is what is termed a spread. The spread encompasses the brokerage services, transaction fees, service costs, and profit margin. Usually, pips are for representing spread in percentage, to a four-decimal place currency quote. The following are the main types of spreads in the Forex market.

Forex markets

A fixed spread is when the difference between ask and bid price is kept constant and not influenced by fluctuations caused by market conditions. They are retained by financial firms for their regularly traded accounts.

A fixed spread with extension is where some quantities can be forecast at a fixed level, while others can be tactically changed depending on the dominant market conditions.

A variable spread vacillates depending on market conditions. Usually, a variable spread is low when the market is relatively quiet (one-two pips) but when the market is more unpredictable (40-50 pips) the spread is much wider. Variable spread is an indication of the market's situation and produces trade uncertainty. This means that devising a strategy becomes more difficult. However, the chance of a high rate of return is greater with the higher level of risk, in comparison with the fixed variable that is more dependable and reliable, but with a much smaller rate of return.

Bid and Ask [Sell and Buy] Definitions

The bid price is the price a market or trader is willing to pay for a certain currency pair in the Forex markets. In other words, it is the price traders will buy their base currency to trade in the Forex. A Forex bid appears to the left of the Forex currency quote. For example, EUR/USD 1.2342/27: the bid price is 1.2342.

The Forex ask price is that which the market will sell a trading currency pair at. It is the price written at the right of a Forex quote.

Majors

Some currencies are known as majors because these are the most commonly traded currencies worldwide. These major currencies are Swiss Franc (CHF), Australian dollar (AUD), Japanese Yen (JPY), Euro (EUR), US Dollar (USD), and Great British Pound (GBP).

Minors

Minor currencies are those whose value is connected to the value of commodities. Countries with these types of currencies usually have a large amount of natural resources to give their currency acquired value. Examples of these resources are gold, diamond, silver, or oil. Examples of minor currencies are Australian Dollar (AUD), Canadian Dollar (CAD), and New Zealand Dollar (NZD).

Exotic Currency

Exotic currencies are those that are rarely traded in the Forex markets. They lack depth, have low trade volumes and are not very liquid. Trading in exotic currencies is expensive as the bid-ask prices and spread are so large.

Exotic currencies are not counted as major currencies in the Forex because of their trading volumes, as they are not easily traded in a typical brokerage account. Examples of exotic currencies in the Forex markets are Thai baht, Iraqi dinar, and Uruguayan Peso.

Trading Metals

The value of precious metals provides clues as to the economic situation of financial markets because they are considered as safety nets during difficult periods in the economy. The need for precious metals isn't determined by geography and so experienced investors branch out their portfolio by trading in them and hedge their bets when the financial markets are weak.

Time-frames

Calendar charts should not be viewed as a strategy component, but rather as a measure of the period of time that has been profitably traded. A point worth noting is that not all traders can avail of the full eight hours of trading daily, as they might have alternative jobs that take up the majority of their time as well as needing to sleep, eat and spend time with their families etc.

This leaves very little time to check the time-frame charts and instead it is more beneficial to inspect the five-minute chart scalping.

Multiple Time Frame Analysis

An experienced trader will make use of several time-frames to observe the trends in a single currency pair in order to form an opinion on the long-term, medium and short-term performance of that pair. This makes use of the multiple time-frames concept.

This approach enables traders to gain a view of the overall direction of the market and currencies, and to find trade setups based on the smaller time-frame charts. This will qualify the Forex traders to make informed decisions on whether to buy, sell or hold trading depending on the overall market direction and so avoid heavy losses.

Automation and All Time-frames

Traders, who are prevented from trading for whatever reason during an important period, can make use of a technological advancement known as customised trading robots.

These trading robots can make use of a computer program set to open and close at the required times five days a week for 24 hours a day. Once open, the robots can assess the market and determine the best times to trade or to hold. This maximises traders' efficiency levels and minimises the time they need to spend actually trading.

Difference in Spread price between currency pairings

Estimated trading volumes in the volatile financial markets are more than $5 trillion meaning that secure spreads are the preferred model of trading between banks and interbank markets. Banks prefer to quote modest rates with narrow spreads to their corporate and government clients. Retail customers, however, prefer a very different approach. Their spread between ask and bid price for a currency pair is often fairly large. As most regulations do not control this market speciality, spread can differ dramatically from one trader or Forex dealer to the next. In this section of the market, the difference rates directly affect the traders, and so it is in their best interest to obtain the optimum exchange rate. The following will explain how the exchange rate is calculated and how sole traders translate this information to generate profits.

Bid-Ask Spread

Comprehending bid and ask spreads is straightforward as it is simply the difference between the price at which a Forex trader buys and then sells a currency pair.

It is usually the price the trader is ready to pay or bid for a currency pair and then the price that they are willing to sell the currency for. The difference between these forms of the Bid-Ask spread.

Direct and Indirect Currency Quotes

A direct quote, or price quotation, conveys the amount of unit currency regarding the domestic currency. An indirect currency quote, or volume quotation, is a direct reciprocal of a direct quote and conveys the foreign currency per unit of domestic currency.

Currency Rate and Cross Currencies

When trading in cross currency rates it is important to have some knowledge regarding the quoting mechanism. The conditions concerning cross currency rates include the expressing price of one currency in terms of another currency, not the US dollar. Global travellers would experience a lot of cross currency as they travel across continents, changing currencies as they go.

What is a Forex Pair?

A Forex pair is a quotation in the price structure of currencies traded in the money markets. The value of a single currency is derived from the comparison of another currency, and together they form a Forex pair. The first currency that appears in a pair is called the base currency, while the second is called the quote currency. Here are some of the main currency pairs in the world. A quotation in the price structure of pairs of currencies traded in the Forex markets is known as a Forex pair. The worth of one currency is calculated by comparing it against another currency and this creates a Forex pair. The base currency is the first one to appear in the pair and the second is known as the quote currency. Some of the world's main currency pairs are as follows: EUR/USD; USD/CAD; USD/JPY; GBP/USD; and USD/CHF.

What is a Lot?

A lot is equal to 100,000 units of the base currency in the Forex markets. This standard is considered trade size and there are three main categories of lots: mini-lot; micro-lot; and standard lot.

Lot in Trading

A standard lot has an order of 100,000 units. Currency pairs are traded in units of 100,000 regular lots; 10,000 is a micro lot and this means the buying or selling of the base currency while selling or buying an equivalent number of the other currency in the pair.

Types of Lot Accounts

As the Forex groundwork has been explained, the following will expand on that knowledge into economic news and more detailed trading techniques in the Forex markets. There are Various types of trading accounts and, before deciding on a broker, it is important to know a bit about the background of each. An individual would be best advised to choose an account that is reliant on risk tolerance. Other factors that need to be taken into account are the amount of the initial investment and the time available for actual trading per day.

Standard Accounts

The most common account is the standard account, which allows traders access to trade many different currencies, each worth \$100,000. To clarify, a trader does not need to invest \$100,000 of capital in order to start trading as, due to the essential rules of margin and leverage, an investor can trade with amounts as low as \$1,000.

Mini Trading Accounts

A mini trading account is one with the amount of \$10,000 and permits Forex traders to participate in trading with smaller lots. A regular account is ten times this and so many brokers offer mini accounts to interest a greater number of clients. It is particularly suited to those clients who wish to experiment in the markets before committing larger amounts of money. Standard or regular accounts require large sums of money, which most new traders do not have.

Managed Trading Account

Managed trading accounts are unusual outside of high net worth individuals, where the accounts are offered as an overall wealth management strategy. The principal invested for trade is owned by investors but managed by a team of financial professionals. They make the decisions on whether and when to buy and sell in the Forex markets. The account managers manage the accounts, as stockbrokers administer the stock accounts. However, the investor decides the profit targets and risk management guidelines for the account.

Copy Trading Accounts

A copy trading account is a type of trading account that enables a trader to automatically replicate the trades of another trader, a practice commonly referred to as mirror trading. The process works as follows: the trader, known as the "copier", selects a more experienced trader, referred to as the "signal provider", whose trades they wish to follow. Once the selection is made, the copier's account automatically mirrors the signal provider's trades, including both the amount and the timing of each transaction. This system allows the copier to benefit from the experience and expertise of the signal provider, potentially enhancing their trading outcomes.

ECN Broker

ECN brokers are those specialists who use electronic communication networks (ECN) to provide access to their clients to other players in the Forex markets. As the ECN broker has wider access, they are able to provide a combination of price quotations from multiple market participants. This allows them to offer their clients ask/bid prices and spreads that they would not otherwise be able to access in the market.

Understating an ECN Broker

As the function of an ECN broker is to match trading members in the Forex markets, it is not permissible for them to trade against their clients. To do so would be in breach of standard procedure. As the spreads utilised by ECN brokers are lower than the standard, they are able to charge their clients a set commission amount per transaction. It is necessary to note that an ECN broker can only enable a trade for involved investors on electronic communication networks.

This is not an issue, however, and choosing this type of broker is commonly undertaken as they charge lower fees and provide extra trading times.

Calculating PIP Value

The example illustrated below has assumed the value of one pip as 10,000 EUR/USD, where the base currency is the US dollar. The example below has taken the value of one pip to be 10,000 EUR/USD, with the US dollar as the base currency.

1. Multiplying 10,000 by 0.001 (10,000*0.001) is the standard set up for all pairs (except the Japanese Yen pairs).
2. As standard a pip is equal to $1, which is valued against the second pair, or counter currency.
3. Further, in the example, we are using EUR/USD, so USD is used as the counter pair, but one pip is worth $1

for a 10k of EUR/USD. In this example, EUR/USD is used so USD is the counter pair but one pip is worth $1 for a $10k of EUR/USD.

To further learn how to calculate the value of a pip when your base value is not similar to the second currency pair, check the example below where all calculations are indicated. Besides, the example shows how you compute the value of one pip for 1-10k lot of EUR/GBP where the base currency is USD. The examples below are provided to demonstrate how to calculate the value of a pip, especially when the base value is not the same as the second currency pair. The examples also show how to calculate the value of one pip for 1-10k lot of EUR/GBP where USD is the base currency.

i. Start by multiplying 10,000*0.0001 as 1/10,000 is standard for all currency pairs (except the Japanese Yen).
ii. Each pip is worth $1 and is used as the counter currency. In this example EUR/GBP is being used and GBP is the counter currency of the currency pair above.
iii. Therefore, take the prevailing exchange rate of the GBP/USD, multiply it by one and calculate the value of one pip according to the base currency.
iv. In the example indicated above, GBP/USD is trading at $1.66, and one pip for EUR/GBP is equivalent to USD 1.66.

DIFFERENT TYPES OF TRADERS

Scalper Trader

Scalper traders (or skimmers) are so called because of the speculative methods they assume in the Forex markets. The core of their methods is to 'skim to scoop' regular smaller profits from multiple trade scenarios each day. Scalper traders will usually open their trading stance and close it on the same day. They do not maintain their trading position into another trading session or hold it in overnight trading.

Scalpers are not steady, continuous traders like other more regular traders. They grab opportunities when it suits themselves and will quickly open and close their trade on a particular scenario. Day traders usually choose to trade off five-minute and 30-minute charts, while a scalper will trade off one-minute charts for obtaining several smaller profits. The main goal of a scalper trader is to capture the high-velocity moves on the release of economic information and to take advantage of the variable market interests.

Personality of a Scalper Trader

Scalping is not a method that can be assumed by any trader. Skimmers usually have very specific personality traits, enabling them to make daring trading decisions at short notice. They need to have obsessive levels of concentration as they cannot afford to miss any information displayed during a trading session. Their window of opportunity could be mere seconds in order to obtain their multiple small profits. As well as having to fiercely concentrate for long periods of time, a skimmer must be able to take in all of the information and, within seconds, make a decision quickly. It must be almost an instinctual thing, as they do not have the time to leisurely absorb, analyse and decide on their next move.

This instantaneous decision-making ability is at the heart of a successful scalper trader. Their tactics are not based on in-depth analysis and extensive studying of the market conditions. Their talent lies in being able to see a favourable opportunity in the market and having the fortitude to act on it. Therefore, the scalper trader can be described as having a personality based on thriving on market instability and being able to make a decisive snap decision based on the ability to read those conditions.

Market Making and Scalping

Scalpers and market makers have a similar effect on the distribution of commerce. When choosing a particular trading position, what a market maker is really doing is aiming to offset that position and to obtain spread from that session. Scalpers and market makers have different purposes in the financial markets and market makers trade consistently throughout the day. This does not, however, include bank traders who trade on behalf of their banks.

There are several differences between a market maker and a trade scalper that are worth noting. Basically, market makers get the spread while a scalper pays the spread. In other words, a market maker will earn the spread, but a scalper pays the spread during trading. As a result of this, when a scalper trader purchases currencies at the asking price and sells it on at the bid price, they have to wait for the market to move substantively to cover the spread they have paid.

A market maker, however, sells on the asking price and purchases on the bid price. This creates an instant pip or two profit margin because they generated the market. The overall result of this is that although both types of traders aim to quickly and regularly get in and get out of a trading session, market makers will more likely break even during their trading sessions as opposed to the scalpers.

Market makers, however, look favourably on when scalpers participate in the market as the more they trade, the more spread they pay. This means that the more that scalpers trade, the more a market maker will profit as they earn one or two pips from each spread that scalpers pay.

Pros and Cons of Scalping

Scalping, as can be guessed from the name, is a rapid method of training where traders profit from their ability to make fast, accurate decisions. Scalping, as a strategy, is the optimum one for a person who can observe a trading action and can concentrate on one- or two-minute charts. The following are some of the advantages of scalping traders:

i. A scalper can make a quick profit from trading every day in the Forex markets;
ii. Scalpers are not encumbered by extensive examination of the markets or evaluation of the information to make their decisions.
iii. A scalper makes their profits through control over market fluctuations and instability and not through market forces.

Cons

i. An obvious disadvantage is that scalpers can only make small profits per trade, due to the nature of how they operate.
ii. Scalpers also encounter very high costs of business as covering the costs of their spread can only occur when the market appreciates. This is in contrast to other traders who earn their profits from trade spread.

iii. A scalper trader is not considered a professional in the financial markets as their skill is at detecting market volatility and not in reading other market indicators.

Starting up Scalp trading

To establish a scalp trading business you require excellent observational skills, solid access to information on the activities of market makers, rapid internet connection, and a platform on which to facilitate rapid buying and selling of trade stances. The trade platform needs to have buttons for buying and selling currency pairs so that the trader can just click the correct button when necessary. These buttons need to be in place as sometimes implementing a decision takes split seconds and could mean the difference between making a profit or a loss.

Day-Trader

Day traders are distinctive because they participate in both long and short trade sessions. Their goal is to gain profit through highlighting the intraday instability as a result of momentary incompetence in the demand and supply for currency in the market. There are no open trade sessions overnight and so a trader must close all trading sessions at the end of each day. Day traders can also use their market power to boost the profits they earn from slight price movements in the Forex market.

Activities of the Day Traders

Day traders are constricted in their activities by the bid-ask spreads on offer in the market. Trading commissions and the costs for the real-time feeds and financial analysis cause them further difficulties as these heavily impact their operation costs. A wide range of knowledge and familiarity for the market are needed for day traders to be successful in their day-to-day business, which are vital for spotting the optimum times to trade. To succeed, day traders not only need these skills but also extensive financial knowledge in order to guarantee profit.

There are many methods available that can be adopted by traders to assist them in making stronger trading judgements that lead to profit. Electronic trading systems capable of analysing the market to calculate the best trading opportunities and other more instinctual systems are available to day traders to assist them in their daily business.

Items Traded by Day Traders

Forex investors make use of extensive data analysis to verify the future developments of a company and invest their money based on this analysis. Day traders, however, concentrate on informed market scrutiny of the varying interest rates in the market. Investors' security is based on their level of precise decisions made on the long-term prospects of a company, but day traders derive their security levels from price action traits instead of performance.

A day trader relies on the variations in price in the market and the average daily range per day. A day trader can only experience security when there are enough price variations in a normal trading session. The optimum tactic for a day trader is to seize price movements and to determine the best time to buy and sell in the money markets.

A day trader is also focused on the liquidity and volumes of pairs traded in the market while entering and exiting the market. Small profits are obtained through the regular entry and exiting of the market per trading session. It is important to note, however, that capital market securities with their minimal daily range and low trade volumes are inappropriate for consistent trading.

How Day Traders Engage in Daily Trade

Day traders prefer to operate within any event that occurs with short-term market movements. News-led trading is a common and widespread method among day traders and allows them to gain small profits. Scheduled, significant pronouncements based on topics such as economic information, corporate profits or central bank interest rates cause heightened potential, and day traders can take advantage of this to maximise their profits. When the outcome does not match the expectations or exceeds it, however, operators try to make the most of the situation.

Another common method includes fading the gap at the start of each trading session. If the opening prices show a gap regarding the previous day's trading, then choosing a tactical stance in the reverse direction is known as fading the gap. On those days where there are vital news events or gaps, day traders will need to make their decisions at the start of the day as to what direction they are going to take. If the market shows signs of an upward direction, then day traders buy securities that demonstrate strength when their values fall. When the market falls, day traders will buy short-term securities that are weak when their prices recover. Unfortunately, there are as many day trading methods and techniques as there are actual day traders, because each has devised and developed their own methods in order to stay ahead of the pack and both maximise profits while guaranteeing some level of security.

Pros of Day Traders

i. It is possible to make considerable profits with this method;
ii. Day traders are autonomous and are not reliant on anyone for their profits;
iii. Day trading is exciting and fast-paced.

Cons of Day Trading

i. Risk of extensive losses of capital funds;
ii. Huge start-up and operational costs incurred.

Final Take on Day Trading

Day trading is a complicated talent to acquire as it calls for endurance, persistence and restraint. It is common knowledge that the majority of new day traders have a high three-month failure rate. Time spent observing and learning from an experienced, successful trader is beneficial to becoming successful, and routine practice and constructive assessment of progress is also important for improvement. A sound strategy is for a day trader to set a maximum figure of loss that they can suffer in a day, to ensure that they do not experience negatively impacting their financial status in the business. Reaching this low point is an indication that it is time to stop, unless the trader can see a certain play to make to ensure making a profit. Maintaining this cut-off point can be the difference between success and failure.

Swing traders

Swing traders are highly capable of using their excellent technical analysis skills combined with extensive basic information to obtain at a considerable price. They are extremely efficient in avoiding periods of down-time in market trading. They have an extremely capable use of capital and are able to achieve a fairly high return on capital invested. On the downside, however, they charge much higher commission rates and they are riskier and more variable in their returns than other methods of Forex trading.

Forex trading

Swing trading can be difficult for the standard retail trader. Clients who choose these types of professional traders know that they will have access to wide-ranging experience, impact on the market, greater access to reliable, useful information and the ability to trade in large amounts of capital investment. However, they will also have limited access to instruments they are allowed to trade in.

Swing traders specialise in their knowledge of swing stocks, currencies and securities that occur within a few days. This means that they can take a few days or weeks to carry out a single transaction and to identify if it made a profit or a loss. In comparison to day traders, swing traders base their function on participating in the Forex markets based on the size of capital needed and the intensity of the trade periods.

Pre-Market

The working day for a swing trader starts at 6am EST, ahead of the market's opening bell. This period before the bell is rung is to allow the traders to obtain a feel for the day's market situation and to identify any possible trading instruments and currency pairs, to formulate a market checklist and to assess any active trade positions.

Market Synopsis

The first order of the day for a proficient swing trader is to brief themselves on the news or any important events that have occurred in the financial markets. This briefing needs to cover topics such as inflation directions, interest rates of currencies and global trading events. This should be followed by an update on the sector attitudes in the Forex market and finally the swing traders need to investigate current holdings on issues such as earnings and SEC filings.

Finding Potential Trades

Once this is done, swing traders can turn their attention to skimming through the information for the best possible daily trades. Normally, a swing trader will only agree to a trading decision with the incentive of a key stimulus and when they can administer or leave the position through the use of technical analysis to their benefit. Two methods that swing trades are incentivised are:

i. Exceptional opportunities. These usually occur following SEC filings or noteworthy news bulletins. Examples of these can include initial public offers, insider buying, or mergers and acquisitions. Swing traders find this information through constant observing of the various SEC filings, which are vital for providing an edge in the market. Conscientious traders can benefit from huge rewards from their informed decisions, although there are high levels of risk involved too. This is why swing traders buy when others are selling, and sell when others are buying. This is known as 'fading' to break from the over-exuberant responses to events and news.

ii. Market sector players. Swing traders can identify opportunities through analysis of news and by referring to reliable sources of information on sector plays that are showing a strong performance. For example, if a swing trader can determine the performance of the energy sector by perusing exchange-traded funds, they can identify a high-risk, high return venture in which to invest their capital.

These market sector player openings are difficult to recognise but have a high rate of returns compared to many other opportunities available to swing traders. In summary, a swing trader profits from buying promising trends at the right time, staying with these trends until they show signs of decline and then selling at a profit.

Watch List

A swing trader's watch list can decide the success or failure of their business. It needs to contain reliable detailed information on the Forex stocks as these determine those trades that will ensure a high rate of returns. This watch list can be as rudimentary as an erasable white board on which to list the specific, organised prospects, stop-loss prices and the target prices of multiple stock markets.

Monitoring Present Trade Positions

Before the market's opening bell rings, it is vital that swing traders continuously examine the performance of current positions. Prior to acting on any promising positions, they then need to assess any relevant news headlines to make sure there is nothing dramatic about to happen that may alter their position. Usually, traders can ascertain this by typing their stock symbols into a news article, and the results should show them any latest updates on the stock.

Online the traders can check for any recent filings by searching the SEC's EDGAR database. All stock information needs to be analysed, even if it does not directly influence their current trading position, as this may change in the future. Swing traders are also flexible enough to change their position in the event of a possible profit or loss.

Merits of a Swing Trader

1. This method is simple to grasp and easy to participate in, in contrast to the previous two methods;

2. Traders are able to easily calculate their profits and are flexible enough to take precautions against losses;
3. Swing traders are recognised as professionals and can make a full-time career out of their activities.

Disadvantages of a Swing Trader

1. A large sum of start-up capital is necessary to participate in profitable trading;
2. Swing traders need to constantly stay abreast of current affairs in order to profit from their pursuits;
3. Swing traders can only access certain levels of the Forex markets and so are limited to the stocks and securities they are allowed to trade in.

The Position Trader

A Forex trader who maintains a specific position for several months, or until they profit from it, is known as a position trader. This type of trader is interested in the long-term view and less concerned with any day-to-day fluctuations in the market. Their stance is that, long-term, everything will work out for the best.

Therefore, a position trader needs to watch the markets to make sure that they reach their trade goals. Such goals can include holding out for a currency pair or security to reach a specified value, or delaying selling stock until there is a new stock split in the market.

Operations of a Position Trader

Even though a position trader concentrates on the long-term profits from a stock, it is necessary to keep up-to-date on possible trends through monthly updates. This is the main difference between day trading, as they are involved with short-term market fluctuations, while position trading is more concerned with long-term trade objectives.

Why do Traders Take Positions in the Market?

A trader can take a position based on their overall business strategies or simply on a speculative basis. An example would be where an investor buys Euros, speculating that the Euro will appreciate in value sometime in the future.

This means that the incentive for taking a particular trade position is based on the conviction of a possible direction instead of firm market facts. This could be because they have certain information that is not common knowledge, regarding the Euro. The investor will therefore take this position, until it comes about.

Taking a position in Forex trading involves holding that position until such a time as it is beneficial for them to close that position at a profit, or at a minimum, to a predetermined limit loss. A 'hedge' is when a business maintains an extended position to enter into an offsetting position. A hedge position provides a barrier to the market to prevent moves that could damage a position before it can be closed.

Spot positions Vs. Future Position

A spot position is one that is taken for certain instant results. This type of position could show returns in a matter of one or two business days, reliant on any risks or securities involved. The cost of a position is agreed on the transaction date, not the payment date, which might occur several days later. Any transactions that take longer than a spot transaction are classed as a future or forward position. Likewise, a future transaction value is agreed on the day that the deal is made but the payment date can be days, weeks, months or even years into the future.

Options of a Position Trader

Position traders have the freedom to take positions on a variety of buying and selling options: they are not limited to just stock trading. A call option is considered the best choice as it is not taken as a commitment to buy securities or currencies at a specific price or at a specific time. The permission to sell a security is known as a put option. Traders can decide on a position in the underlying securities or currency to sell the call or put options. Traders can then let their option expire or sell or buy, depending on what is beneficial to them themselves.

These are only a few types of traders. Each trader is an individual in their methods and tactics and can follow the plan best suited to their overall profit goal. Each type of trader analysed above has their own pros and cons that make them distinctive in their modes of operation and reason for being chosen in the markets. Overall, flexibility would be the key determinant of a trader's ability to triumph as it is their reaction to a situation that decides their levels of success.

HOW FUNDAMENTALS AFFECT FOREX

Interest Rates

Market interest rates are some of the most important factors in the Forex market because they are the base for traders to earn profits from their transactions. Interest rates change as a result of economic markers in the market and are increased or decreased by the eight main central banks. Unexpected changes in interest rates can heavily affect traders who can earn large profits or suffer massive losses depending on the direction in which they go.

The reaction time of individual operators can make all the difference on the profit volumes a trader can earn from their actions.

Interest rates are vital to traders because if the interest rates on a set pair of currencies traded on the Forex market are high, the trader will receive greater profits from buying and selling that pair. This may seem like an easy way to make money, but the inflation imposed on that set pair of currencies can cancel out the benefits of the higher interest rates and result in losses to the trader. Experience and skill regarding the functions of interest rates and their effects can help traders make informed decisions regarding investments and preventing losses. The following are a few technical pointers every trader should be aware of prior to commencing investment:

i. Dollar interest rates are increased by the FED rate. The value of a currency is controlled by interest rates and the general economic conditions in a country. Central banks will usually raise interest rates when the economy shows strong and steady growth in order to prevent currency inflation. As interest rates rise, yields on assets traded on that currency rise, which increases the demand for that currency.

   An increase in the demand for a currency encourages traders to purchase other currencies using the dollar to diversify out the currency pairs they are willing to trade on the Forex markets.

ii. An increase in interest rates can sometimes stimulate closing trades. New traders need to be aware of an emergent trade of the dollar that has damaged trade and liquidity in the Forex markets of developing countries. The dollar situation is so fragile that any rise in FED interest rates can negatively affect the carry dealers. These dealers depend on suppositions based on the borrowing of the US dollar and investing that money on high yielding currency pairs in the market. As a result, when these currencies reduce in value against the dollar because of rises in interest rates, the actual gains are balanced by losses in foreign exchange, which leads to trade closing.

Housing Market trends and Forex Markets

As the housing market expanded and was joined by a greater number of real-estate dealers, the level of rivalry among the numerous traders resulted in lower interest rates. Banks normally obtain the majority of their revenue from the interest paid on mortgages and asset financing loans. When millions of real-estate developers flood the market, it becomes next to impossible for banks to make any significant profits.

As a result, banks need to introduce low interest rates to survive in the face of competition from those real-estate developers. Money lenders only obtain low interest rates in comparison to the amounts they pay out on deposits. The housing market, therefore, can heavily influence the financial markets because the banks receive less interest for the money they lend, as opposed to the interest they need to pay on deposits, which have dramatically reduced.

Countries that have experienced unstable conditions in their housing market have placed extreme pressure on their currencies, which leads to a poor performance in the global money markets.

Role of inflation on the money market

Historically, inflation has long been a deterrent to the growth of a country's economy because a strong economic growth rate is only reached when the economic growth rates surpass the inflation rate. The main role of a central bank is to regulate inflation and it does this through constant revision of its monetary policies. This means that the policies adopted by the central banks have a direct influence on the value of the currency, which has a knock-on effect on the Forex market.

Currency exchange rates can be negatively affected if inflation is not closely monitored and traders will be hesitant to trade in it. Traders can get a negative impression of the currency, which means low volumes of that currency are traded, which reduces the value of that currency against the other major currencies. When a currency has low purchasing power its money market performance is negatively affected, and this leads to low profit margins.

If the domestic currency weakens then importing goods into that country becomes expensive because the price of foreign products increases. As a result, the central bank of that country usually increases the interest rates to dampen the negative effect of inflation on the currency. Alternatively, a strong currency reduces inflation and so the central bank will reduce the interest rates to counteract the currency from becoming too strong.

Therefore, inconsistent interest rates are caused by inflation, but these are a positive effect in the Forex markets. However, high inflation rates discourage traders from trading in that country's currency due to its reduced demand despite the higher interest it earns. In comparison, a stable currency has reduced interest rates, which means lower profits and a low demand for it among traders. This demonstrates the importance of knowledge of inflation rates for various currencies for traders so that they can make informed decisions on whether to buy or sell their currency.

Economic Growth

GDP is defined as the total amount of all goods and services generated by the companies in a country, as well as what is produced by all of the international companies operating within its borders. DDP is a gauge of the rate at which the country's economy is expanding. This is more important. DDP is used by traders to verify the growth of a country, and GDP is used to estimate the currency value.

Indicators of economic growth in the GDP are industrial manufacture, purchasing managers' index, producer price index, consumer price index and actual sales figures. Specific indicators can test the success of their corresponding economic sectors. For example, the housing market is a vital indicator of the state of the financial market.

Currency interest rates are some of the most important factors governing the Forex market. The central bank controls the base rate, and this is the base for the money market. Base rates are used to manage the economy because banks use them to determine the interest rates that they will charge their clients.

Base rates can also be used to manage inflation as they can be lowered to encourage growth or increased to avoid depreciation of the domestic currency.

Banks are the main participants in the Forex markets, and if changes occur in interest rates which reduce their ability to lend money then the domestic currency is put under pressure to preserve its value against stronger currencies.

The expectations of Forex traders can increase the pressure on the domestic currency, particularly when they expect that the central bank is about to increase the interest rate. This will cause the traders to buy large sums of currency and hold on to it until they can sell it on for a profit. These economic growth activities put pressure on the value of the domestic currency, which can lead to artificial shortfalls in the currency, which cause a further reduction in its value. Changes in interest rates and growth in the economy are vital occurrences in the market and can determine whether traders will trade in the domestic currency or not.

Countries whose economic growth has plateaued can only offer small interest rates and traders will not trade in their currencies as they will only earn small profits. Developing countries that are showing strong signs of growth are ideal for traders who have correctly predicted this growth and can benefit from the profits arising from their predictions. As the GDP of a country is used by central banks as the basis for deciding the base interest they will charge banks for money lending, then if a central bank increases its interest rate then this increases the amount of interest the borrower has to repay. This may mean a decrease in loans and the flow of money in the economy, which could contract economic growth because many industrial sectors have a high requirement for financing to expand. Therefore, variations on the GDP have a direct influence on both currency value and profit margins available to traders.

Job Data

Employment rate data on a country are a clear gauge of that country's economic growth rate. A country that can provide jobs to its population is considered to have a strong economic growth rate because they will have increased purchasing capabilities. This data can be skewed, however, as countries like Asia, for example, can show that employment levels are high, but the workers are paid a pittance and are living in poverty at less than a dollar per day.

Job data can influence the economic growth rate in several ways. The first is by monitoring the total jobs provided by the economy and the unemployment level. New jobs created in an economy is an indicator of the strength of the economy and is observed closely by Forex traders. If a large number of jobs are generated, this could be a sign that the economy is expanding. However, traders need to determine the industry that the jobs are created in, the overall population and if the population has sufficient education levels to take up the jobs.

If a country has a high unemployment rate it is generally assumed that that country is going through an economic downturn. Again, this may not be an accurate reflection of the actual status, as low unemployment could mean that the country has nearly full employment. In this case the interest rates will probably increase, which will benefit the Forex traders.

This shows how the Forex traders need to gather more accurate data, and not just jump to conclusions. Background information, such as population size, literacy levels, and the employment rate of the country need to be determined before positions are decided on as assumptions could lead to miscalculations about the state of the economy and heavy losses incurred by the traders.

Crude Oil

The crude oil industry and the currency market have been closely linked for decades and fluctuations in one have repercussions for the other. These corresponding reactions are of great interest to Forex traders. Some of the main factors that they need to keep track of are the distribution of resources, market psychology and balance of trade between countries, regions, and continents. These are the factors that maintain the links between crude oil prices and the currency market.

Crude oil can also dramatically influence the devaluation of the currency and the inflation of a country. This is due to the global importance for oil as both a raw material and as a source of fuel. Crude oil prices are usually stated in US dollars per barrel. This results in increased pressure for the dollar when crude oil prices increase, so central banks have to increase interest rates and issue more dollars in order to avoid a market emergency. Countries that are heavily dependent on their vast oil reserves are very aware of the relationship between oil and currency, and recognise that any changes in the price of oil will have an effect on their financial markets.

Countries that have a heavy reliance on imported crude oil feel the pressure when oil prices increase, and this has an effect on the price of all of their necessities and cost of fuel. Most countries have tried to maintain oil reserves to protect their economies from dramatic variations in oil prices, but assembling the infrastructure necessary to store this is costly and has impacted the dollar as countries have needed to borrow heavily to pay for this infrastructure. This heavy level of borrowing has contracted economic growth and this along with crude oil shortages have caused a crisis in the world's economies.

Recent issues with sales have increased the likelihood of deflation of the US dollar and the price of a barrel of oil. This has increased the connection between the two and has had a negative influence on countries without crude oil reserves and the Eurozone countries. Even countries with huge oil mining capabilities have had problems keeping up with countries with huge oil reserves. This demonstrates how important it is for traders to monitor the prices of crude oil and regulations governing them, as these will affect the value of the US dollar and the other major currencies. The discovery of new oil fields is another crucial news topic that traders need to watch out for as this will increase the supply of oil from a region and reduce pressure on the US dollar.

Yield Curve

A yield curve is a display of data that can show the maturity of interest rate for a loan contract. It is usually a government paper given in a specific currency. The curve is created by plotting interest rates against their maturities when borrowing is allowed; the combining values form the yield curve on the graph. In general, the yield curve contains important information but in particular to the Forex markets. Yield curves are used to value government securities, which are considered to be very safe assets as they have maximum liquidity at any given time. The majority of international lenders would examine the yield curves before lending or extending payment due dates, without even examining the state of the borrower. This would enable the lenders to charge a higher interest rate than what they would get from investing in a government paper.

The yield curve is also used as a sign of economic cycles and can demonstrate any pressures a currency is likely to experience. Central bank policies regarding the settlement of several government policies considerably influence the yield curve and directly affect inflation and the currency value of a given country. Prior to an economic recession, the yield curve is inverted, with assets that have shorter maturity periods receiving higher interest rates and shorter periods receiving lower interest rates. Traders need to be able to examine the yield curve data and to make informed decisions based on the information. The yield curve has valuable influence regarding the valuation of a domestic currency and its performance in the Forex markets.

China Factor

Even though it is a developing market, China has immense influence on the currency markets. Its economic activities directly affect the US dollar as the value of the Yuan is linked to it. In 2016, China contributed to 7% of the total transaction in the Forex market, which caused shockwaves throughout the market. As America is China's biggest trade partner, China needs to regulate the value of the Yuan to obtain greater benefits from its exports.

This is because the power of the Yuan is due to China's massive amount of exports to America. The main exports are clothes and machinery.

Many American industries send their raw materials to China for cheap assembly and manufacture of their products. The completed products are regarded as exports as they merit foreign exchange for the Chinese economy. Chinese companies are paid in dollars, lodge this money to banks and exchange it for Yuan to pay their workers' salaries and other day-to-day expenditures. This means that Chinese banks hold a large store of US dollars, which reduces the fund of dollars and prevents inflation of the dollar against the Yuan. This in turn devalues the Yuan and so the central bank needs to devise a method of equalising the two.

To achieve this balance, China's central bank devised a tactic to capitalise its reserves into commodities that are of greater value than even government bonds. To do this, the People's Bank of China linked the value of the Yuan to the reference rate and not the value of the US dollar, which decreased the inflation pressure on the dollar. This was done to guarantee that the value of the Yuan is directed by market forces, although this does create greater market instability. This move did, however, result in the Yuan becoming recognised as an official reserve currency.

China's economic reforms and the introduction of these monetary policies had a tremendous effect on the dollar. As the growth of China's economy slowed, this allowed the dollar to appreciate against the Yuan, which affected the global financial markets and increased the problems China faced in terms of obtaining credit.

Although China is the second biggest centre of stock markets in the world, after the US, it is also the most turbulent market as asset prices can vary by as much as 10% per day. A greater number of traders regularly join the financial markets to boost their retirements as there is no social security benefits system in China. This increases the risk levels in China, making the financial and stock markets extremely volatile.

This meant that the Chinese government had to devise methods of slowing down the economy, so Forex traders need to closely observe the Chinese economy if they want to be successful trading on the US dollar, because changes in one directly impacts the other.

Commodity connection

Traders need to be able to forecast in the Forex markets so as to earn profits and identifying links between two markets can greatly increase their chances of making profits.

Gold

Gold is always considered to be a secure trade choice on the Forex markets, especially relative to the US dollar. Strong trade in gold reduces the demand for the dollar, thus preventing high inflation rates. Although gold and the Forex markets have had a long-term trading history, each market responds differently to it depending on its liquidity levels and internal forces at work. It is important to note that the gold market is much smaller than the Forex market and is heavily reliant on its performance, not the other way around. Despite this, excessive gold price variations have a direct impact on the value of the US dollar. Traders need to be aware of any such variations and the ability to predict these can increase profits.

Copper

Any significant economic growth in a country leads to an increase in the building industry and increases the demand for housing, infrastructure and travel hubs such as airports and stations. This results in an increase in the demand for copper, which in turn impacts the value of the dollar. When the dollar faces increased pressure, it depreciates, and central banks have to step in and introduce calming measures to prevent deficiencies in the economy. These measures provide opportunities for traders to increase their profits by forecasting the dollar's next move.

Commodity research bureau – (CRB) index

For many years, the commodity research bureau (CRB) has led the way on the supply and analysis of data for goods, and forecasts on price directions. These forecasts are released through electronic means such as email or print publications, which are used as guides for calculating price movements of multiple global commodities. Price predictions can overflow into the economy, which can encourage exploratory buying and storing of goods to sell at a later date when the prices have gone up. Due to this, Forex markets are reliant on the CRB publications for information to direct their next position. These positions will determine the value of the dollar and the other major world currencies.

Equities

A successful Forex trader is able to recognise prospective movement in an economy or currency. Certain investors try to identify trade relationships or changes in the GDP and this can be achieved through scrutiny of the equity markets. The market equity markets consist of thousands of firms worldwide that generate multiple reports providing vital information to Forex traders. When reviewing the impact of equities in currency markets, it has to be considered globally. Companies that trade in multiple countries provide equity to the Forex markets, and any insider trading information available on these multi-currency organisations is of enormous benefit as it could help them to identify future supply and demand for a specific currency against the dollar or other major currencies.

Consumer conflict report

A consumer conflict report, or consumer price index, quantifies the degree of change in average prices from a cross section of indispensable goods and services. It provides important pointers on inflation as it demonstrates reliable movements in buying behaviours of the general public. It also relates to the speed at which prices drop or rise for multiple products. These reports are used by central banks to predict inflation increases or decreases of different products or services.

Forex traders use the reports to forecast their next trading position as inflation and deflation influence increases and drops in interest rates. This in turn reduces or increases a trader's chances of profits.

Fundamental personalities of currencies

Currencies have basic characteristics that Forex traders can use to identify whether they are strong or weak. The manner in which a currency is viewed worldwide reflects its value and performance in the financial markets. A currency's personality also consists of its history and its ability to perform during periods of economic crisis. This personality is critical for determining the currency's future trends against the major currencies globally and regional trading partners. For example, Eurozone trading partners have a heavy influence on the personality of the Euro. As a result, resolute Forex traders need to take heed of forceful personalities of currencies in addition to other economic markers. It is beneficial for investors to carry out basic personality analysis of several currencies to determine their future trends and to make informed decisions on what to invest in the short and long-term.

FOREX TECHNICAL

To effectively navigate and understand the Forex market, it is essential to explore the three primary types of analysis that traders utilise to develop new trading ideas and strategies. These analytical methods serve as critical tools for investigating market trends, assessing potential trades, and making informed decisions. The foundational types of analysis in the Forex market include technical analysis, fundamental analysis, and sentiment analysis.

Each approach offers unique insights into market dynamics and price movements. Technical analysis focuses on examining historical price data and chart patterns to predict future movements, while fundamental analysis evaluates economic indicators and news events that can impact currency values. Lastly, sentiment analysis gauges the overall mood of the market and traders' perceptions, helping to understand how market psychology can influence price trends. By familiarising yourself with these three methods, traders can enhance their trading skills and develop a deeper understanding of the complexities within the Forex market.

Fundamental Sentiment

Technical analysis is used as the main method for analysing price movements in trades. By checking previous trends and price changes, a trader can determine the current trading conditions and forecast any future price increases. Technical analysis is reinforced by the premise that the market price reflects the market information. If true, then price movement should be enough information to succeed in trading. 'History repeats itself' would be a common belief here.

There has been much debate regarding the advantages and disadvantages of each type of analysis, but what is in agreement is that comprehensive knowledge of all three must be learned in order to trade effectively in the Forex market. Only focusing on one or two methods is to only gain an uneven view of the market. All three methods are necessary so as to form a complete view. Lack of a complete set of analytical tools could mean that a trader misses opportunities for profits.

Technical

Most of the previous information discussed actually covers technical analysis comprehensively. Historical trades that demonstrated a steady price that held and provided resistance or core support can be treated by traders as an indication of present trade capabilities.

Previous price information can be used as an indication of future price information and technical analysts can use this to formulate their current trade positions with the expectation that the status quo won't change.

Charts are the tools most commonly found in technical analysis in the Forex markets. They are an easy, visual representation of previous information that are often used by technical analysts.

Precedents and trends can be quickly singled out through analysis of historical data, which can open up new opportunities for trade.

As there is a huge number of traders who mainly use some form of technical analysis method, most statistics and price patterns generally follow a set layout.

The market is likely to demonstrate a repeat of previous trends, due to the ever-increasing volume of traders that make use of charts to identify patterns and trends in prices.

It is important to be aware, however, that technical analysis can have a biased view.

The reason for this is that although several traders may view the same information, each may interpret it in a different way in terms of price direction.

The rudimentary points of technical analysis will be useful when the more intricate aspects such as pivot points, Bollinger, or Fibonacci, are introduced.

At first glance, some of the more advanced features of Forex trading and technical analysis can seem incomprehensible.

However, becoming confident with the basics will ensure greater ease of trading in the Forex markets.

Fundamental

Fundamental analysis covers many external effects on the market. For example, analysing how changes in politics, economic situations, and social situations could influence the demand and supply of several assets. Once the theory behind the model is understood, its benefits become apparent. A first lesson in economics teaches that market prices, or in the case of the Forex market, the exchange rate of currency, is decided by the supply chain and the demand for a product. Therefore, it is easy to obtain an indication of which way prices will go, based on the supply chain model, and demand.

Put simply, fundamental analysis examines several factors to identify their influence and to determine which economies are growing and those that are not. Several factors need to be taken into account in a fundamental analysis to provide a clear picture of an event that may be able to influence the currency exchange and the demand for a country's currency. For example, how high unemployment rates can affect a country's monetary policy and its economy in general.

The historical and future strength and ability to grow a country's economy are the main features examined in fundamental analysis: a strong outlook should signify a strong currency in the future.

This is also applicable to investments as the stronger a country's economy, the greater the chance that it will appeal to foreign investors and businesses. When a country has a positive economic outlook, companies will acquire that currency so that they can buy the products that they need.

Fundamental analysis can be recapitulated as follows:

If a country's economy expands and strengthens, its currency will also grow stronger as demand for it increases. Therefore, the central bank will need to intervene to control inflation rates and growth, and as a result, interest rates could rise.

As interest rates rise, assets available for sale in that currency become more attractive. Investors and traders decide to buy the currency so as to be able to purchase the assets. An increase in the demand for a currency results in a corresponding increase in its value.

The data necessary to influence the currency prices and the reasons why will be explained later on in this book. This information will include how the economy manifests sales in retail and the function of the FED Chairman. In summary, the main point to remember for fundamental analysis is that the economic condition of a country determines the direction its currency could take.

Sentiment

The concept of price action should include all of the accessible information on the market. However, even if it did, each individual trader would decipher it differently and act on it distinctively. In reality, the market works differently.

This difference arises as a result of sentiment analysis. Each trader has his or her own views regarding the market and will not forecast its behaviour in the same way. Similar to the social media network, the financial markets consist of many people participating and impacting the platform. Therefore, the market consists of every trader's input. Regardless of the obtainable information, traders formulate a position based on their experience and attitudes and this is what creates the widespread opinion of the Forex market.

The market, however, moves in its own way: a retail trader can do very little to influence its direction. Unless the trader is Goldman Sachs or George Soros, then a single trader believing that a specific currency is going to go a certain way is not going to be influenced by him or her.

Traders need to keep this in mind and carry out sentiment analysis. Trading strategies need input from how the trader feels about the market, its situation and how the trader's interpretation of these will influence their decisions and position. Traders have the option whether to include sentiment analysis or not – they at least have that!

There is a definite value to a sentiment analysis, and the ability to understand it is important. The benefit of having this tool will be explained later on.

There remains one vital question.

As a trader progresses through the World of Forex trading, they will more than likely experience traders with a single view determination that one specific analysis method is the only one worth knowing. Don't be side-tracked! Each method of analysis is different and has its own merits, and each trader should identify the methods that best suit their approach and tactics. This makes sure that the trader can feel secure and confident with their decisions.

Technical analysis makes use of currency price charts; fundamental analysis examines the economic situation of a country; and sentiment analysis scrutinises the market position and its behaviour in the present to forecast the future.

Although separate methods, the three are linked: sentiment is formulated by factors in fundamentals; and technical examines sentimental; and sentimental is used to create an initial framework for prospective traders.

Although each method is different, using them together is extremely beneficial for traders who want to innovate in the Forex markets. Historical information can be gathered and analysed to formulate new positions and tactics. Together, it is better!

Overlooking or omitting one method could mean that vital information is left out and that means that the overall picture would not be obtained.

Succeeding in the Forex market involves accurate and complete use of the three methods of analysis.

What Analysis Type Is Best for Forex Trade?

The following is a four-step example of how only using one method of analysis can lead to failure in the Forex market.

A trader inspects the charts and identifies a trade opportunity. He gets excited at the thought of all of the money he is about to make and is fully confident that to trade with GBP/USD is the way to go.

When confident of your decision, you then quickly trade advantage of the opportunity and purchase GBP/USD. He is positive of his decision and quickly purchases GBP/USD.

Disaster strikes. The currency goes in the other direction. Without the trader's knowledge, a major UK bank has filed for bankruptcy. This turns the opinion for the UK market in a negative direction and traders trade in a direction that is contrary to his position.

The trader has suffered a huge loss. He returns to the charts, irritated that he was caught only focussing on their information. He omitted to follow procedures in sentimental and fundamental analysis before making his decision.

Candlestick Charts

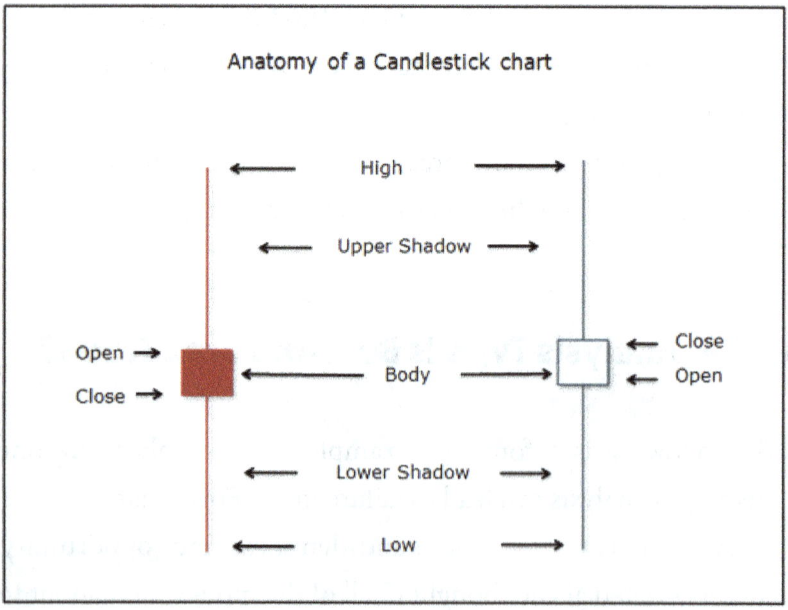

Candlestick Chart Patterns

Candlestick patterns can provide key insights into market sentiment, helping you to predict potential price movements. One of the most significant aspects of reviewing your past trades is your ability to identify these indicators consistently. As you become more familiar with these patterns, it becomes easier for you to spot them during real-time trading, allowing for quicker and more effective responses to market changes.

The Importance of Candlestick Patterns

Candlestick patterns serve as visual representations of price movements and trader behaviour within the market. By analysing these patterns, you can gain a clearer understanding of market trends, reversals, and continuations. Each candlestick represents a specific time frame, and the patterns formed can indicate the prevailing sentiment – whether it be bullish (indicating buying interest) or bearish (indicating selling interest).

Recognising these candlestick patterns can be particularly beneficial for developing your trading strategy. For example, by identifying bullish candlestick patterns, you can capitalise on opportunities where the price is likely to increase. Familiarising yourself with these patterns not only enhances your ability to make profitable trades but also builds your confidence in navigating the forex market more effectively.

Transitioning to Bullish Candlestick Patterns

To begin this journey of recognition, let's focus on bullish candlestick patterns. These patterns typically indicate that buyers are gaining control and that the price of a currency pair is likely to rise. Common bullish patterns include the hammer, the bullish engulfing pattern, and the morning star, among others. Each of these patterns has unique characteristics that signal potential buying opportunities.

For example, when you observe a hammer pattern at the bottom of a downtrend, it suggests that despite selling pressure, buyers have stepped in to push the price higher. Similarly, the bullish engulfing pattern indicates that a larger bullish candle has completely engulfed a smaller bearish candle, signalling a strong shift in momentum towards buying. Recognising these patterns in real-time can significantly enhance your decision-making and trading strategies.

Bullish engulfing pattern

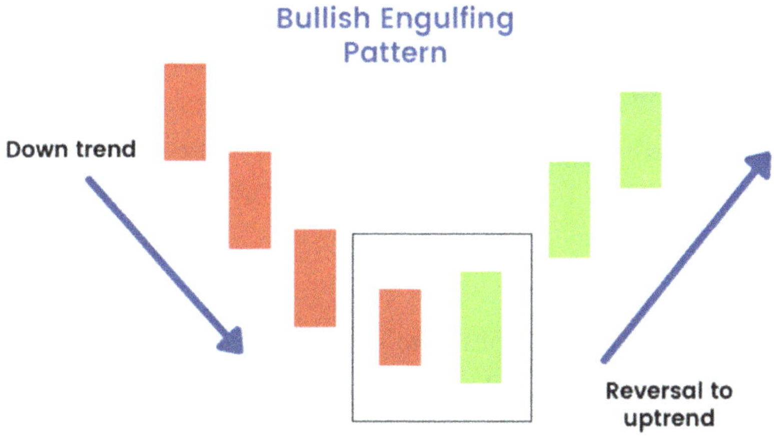

The crucial characteristic of this second candle is that it completely engulfs the body of the first candlestick. This means that the open of the bullish candle is below the close of the bearish candle, and the close of the bullish candle is above the open of the bearish candle.

For example, if you are examining the GBP/USD currency pair, you might first notice a small solid candlestick closing at 1.3000, indicating a certain level of seller strength. The next candlestick forms as a larger hollow candle that opens at 1.2995 and closes at 1.3050. The fact that this bullish candle engulfs the previous solid candle suggests a significant shift in market momentum.

Interpreting the Pattern

The appearance of a bullish engulfing pattern after a bearish trend vehemently suggests that buyers have regained control and that a reversal may be underway. The substantial increase in buying interest, as indicated by the larger hollow candlestick, indicates that traders are becoming more optimistic about future price movements.

This pattern can be particularly effective for you when making trading decisions. The engulfing nature of the pattern communicates that the bulls have overpowered the bears, and as a result, you may consider opening a long position to capitalise on the anticipated price increase.

Practical Application in Trading

When you spot a bullish engulfing pattern, it is wise to look for confirmation before executing a trade. This often means waiting for the next candle to close above the high of the engulfing candle. This confirmation can help ensure that the bullish momentum is sustained.

In the earlier GBP/USD example, if the price action continues with a subsequent candle closing above 1.3050, this would reinforce your decision to enter a long position. You might set your entry point at, say, 1.3055 to ensure you are capturing the upward momentum as the prices rise.

Morning Star

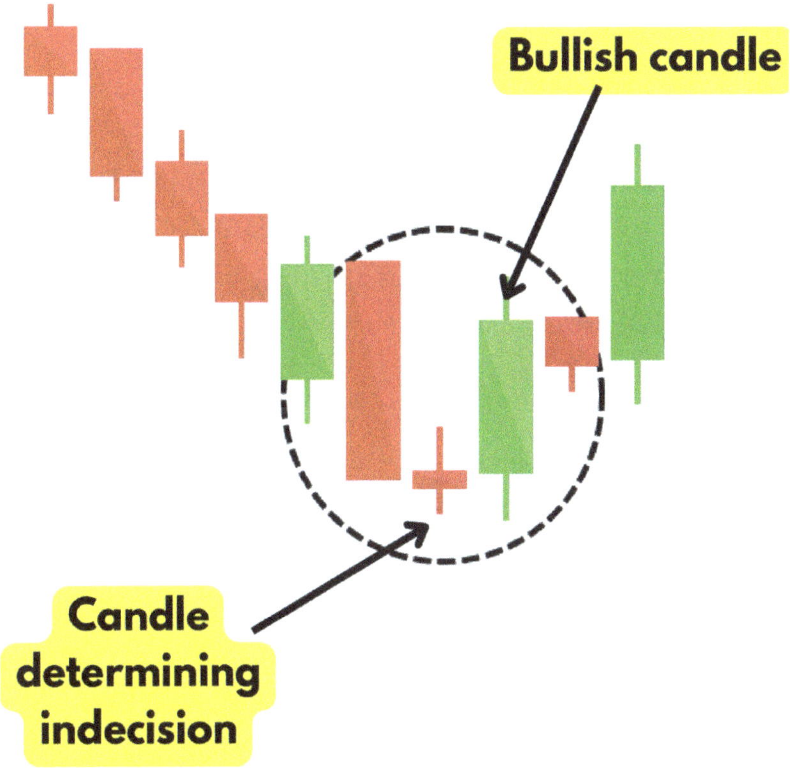

Recognising this pattern can be particularly useful when it appears during a downtrend, as it signals that buying momentum may be returning to the market and that prices could soon begin to rise.

Formation of the Piercing Candlestick Pattern

This pattern consists of two distinct candlesticks, each serving a specific purpose in the formation. The first candlestick is a large red (bearish) candle that indicates strong selling pressure, contributing to the ongoing downtrend. This sizable red candle reflects a period where sellers have dominated the market, pushing prices lower and showcasing a prevailing negative sentiment among traders.

Following this bearish candlestick, the second candlestick forms as a bullish candle.

This candle is characterised by opening with a gap down compared to the close of the previous red candle. Importantly, for the pattern to be validated as a piercing pattern, this bullish candlestick must close above the midpoint of the body of the first bearish candle.

Interpreting the Pattern

When you observe the piercing candlestick pattern, it suggests that buyers have started to gain control of the market despite the recent downtrend.

The significant gap down is indicative of initial selling pressure; however, the bullish candle closing above the 50% mark of the bearish candle's body is a strong signal that buying momentum is increasing. This closing position illustrates a shift in market sentiment, where buyers are overcoming the initial selling pressure and indicating that a reversal may be on the horizon.

For example, imagine that you are analysing the EUR/USD currency pair. You notice that after several weeks of consistently declining prices, a large red candlestick forms, closing at 1.1500. The following day, a bullish candlestick appears, opening at 1.1490 (thus creating a gap down) and then rallying to close at 1.1550. In this case, the second candlestick closes well above the midpoint of the earlier red candle, highlighting the strength of the bullish reversal.

Practical Application in Trading

When trading based on the piercing candlestick pattern, you should consider entering a long position following the confirmation provided by the bullish candlestick. A valid entry point might be placed just above the high of the second candlestick, which signals that upward momentum is likely to continue.

Using the earlier example of the EUR/USD pair, if the bullish candlestick's high is 1.1560, you might set a buy order at 1.1565. Additionally, it is essential to implement sound risk management strategies by placing a stop-loss order below the low of the bullish candlestick. This protective measure helps safeguard your position in case the market reverses unexpectedly.

Engulfing (Bearish)

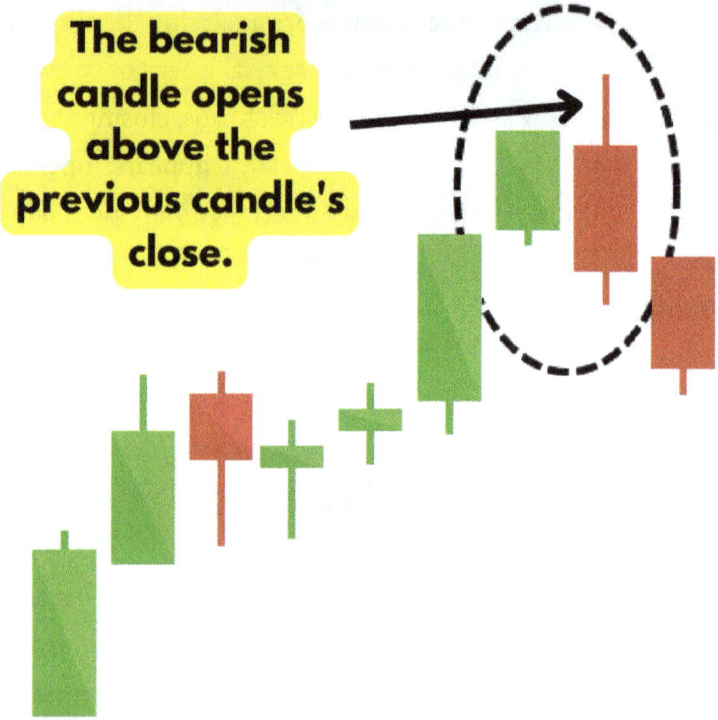

The bearish candle opens above the previous candle's close.

This pattern serves as a critical indicator of a potential reversal in market sentiment, signalling that sellers have gained control over price movements after a period of buying strength.

Formation of the Bearish Engulfing Pattern

A bearish engulfing pattern is characterised by two specific candlesticks. The formation begins with a small hollow candlestick, often referred to as a bullish candlestick, which represents a period of buying activity. Following this small bullish candlestick, a large solid candlestick appears. This second candlestick is bearish, meaning it closes lower than its open, and crucially, it completely engulfs the body of the previous small candle.

This engulfing characteristic is vital. It visually represents a strong shift in momentum, with the larger bearish candle signifying that sellers have decisively taken control of the market. For instance, when a smaller bullish candle, which reflects sustained buying pressure, is followed by a larger bearish candle that fully overlaps and closes below the previous candle's body, it indicates that the buying pressure has been overwhelmed by sellers and that a downward movement may be imminent.

Interpreting the Pattern

In identifying the bearish engulfing pattern, it is crucial to consider the context of the preceding price action. Typically, this pattern emerges after a bullish trend, where buyers have driven prices higher. Once you spot the small bullish candle, the subsequent large bearish candle serves as a warning sign that the bullish momentum is weakening. The buyers, who were previously in control, may be stepping back, allowing sellers to dominate the market.

For example, imagine you are analysing the AUD/USD currency pair on your trading chart.

After a series of upward movements, you notice a small bullish candle that signifies buying activity. Following this, a large bearish candle forms, completely engulfing the smaller candle. This clear transition suggests that sellers have entered the market with significant force, and you might anticipate a subsequent decline in price.

Practical Application in Trading

When observing a bearish engulfing pattern, it can provide a solid signal for your trading decisions. Many traders consider this pattern a strong indication to place a sell order. The optimal entry point is typically set just below the low of the engulfing bearish candle, which confirms that sellers have indeed taken control and that the price is likely to fall further.

For instance, if the AUD/USD currency pair demonstrates this pattern, with the small bullish candle closing at 0.7500 and the larger bearish candle closing at 0.7450, you might decide to initiate a short position slightly below 0.7450.

Inverted Hammer

This candlestick pattern typically emerges at the end of a downtrend, signalling a possible turnaround and an opportunity for you to enter the market at a lower price point before a potential increase.

Formation of the Inverted Hammer Pattern

A key feature of the inverted hammer pattern is its distinctive shape, which is formed by specific characteristics in the candlestick's structure. Similar to the bullish hammer pattern, the inverted hammer consists of a candlestick with a small body.

However, the defining characteristic of the inverted hammer is the long wick that extends above the body of the candlestick. In its classic form, the inverted hammer will have a very small body situated at the bottom of the candlestick, with little to no wick below.

To illustrate, picture a scenario where a currency pair, such as GBP/USD, is experiencing a downtrend. As the price continues to decline, you may notice the formation of an inverted hammer at the bottom of this trend. For instance, the candlestick might open at a price of 1.3000 and trade higher during the session, reaching a peak of 1.3050.

However, by the end of the trading day, the price settles at 1.3010, forming a candlestick with a small body near the lower end of the range and a long upper wick.

Interpreting the Inverted Hammer

When you observe the inverted hammer pattern, especially following a sustained period of price declines, it suggests that buyers have begun to step into the market, attempting to push the price higher. While the price ultimately did not close above the opening level, the long wick indicates that buying pressure was present during the trading period, which could imply a potential reversal is on the horizon.

For example, in the case of the GBP/USD currency pair, the appearance of the inverted hammer could signal that the downtrend may be losing momentum and that there may be a shift towards bullish sentiment. By recognising this pattern, you might consider preparing to enter a long position if a subsequent candlestick confirms the bullish momentum.

Practical Application in Trading

When you trade based on the inverted hammer pattern, it is essential to look for confirmation in the form of a follow-up bullish candlestick. This subsequent candle should ideally close above the high of the inverted hammer. If such confirmation occurs, you may choose to enter a buy order just above this level to capitalise on the anticipated upward movement.

In our earlier example with the GBP/USD pair, if the next candlestick closes at 1.3020, you might decide to place a buy order at 1.3025.

It would be prudent to implement risk management strategies by placing a stop-loss order below the low of the inverted hammer, thus protecting your position should the market move against you.

Piercing Line

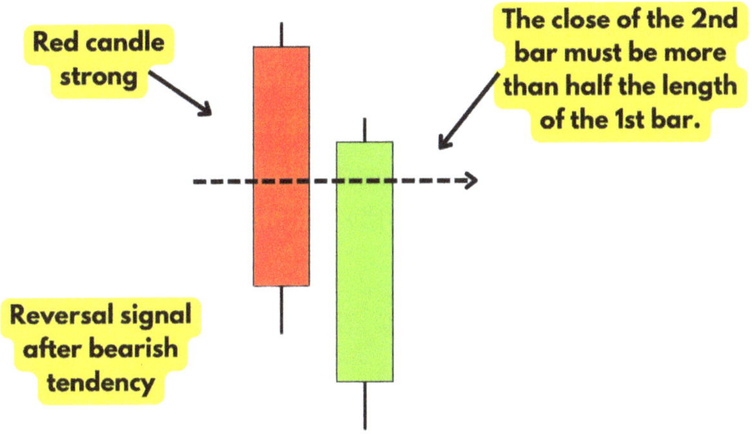
Red candle strong
The close of the 2nd bar must be more than half the length of the 1st bar.
Reversal signal after bearish tendency

Recognising this pattern can be particularly useful when it appears during a downtrend, as it signals that buying momentum may be returning to the market and that prices could soon begin to rise.

Formation of the Piercing Candlestick Pattern

This pattern consists of two distinct candlesticks, each serving a specific purpose in the formation. The first candlestick is a large red (bearish) candle that indicates strong selling pressure, contributing to the ongoing downtrend. This sizable red candle reflects a period where sellers have dominated the market, pushing prices lower and showcasing a prevailing negative sentiment among traders.

Following this bearish candlestick, the second candlestick forms as a bullish candle.

This candle is characterised by opening with a gap down compared to the close of the previous red candle. Importantly, for the pattern to be validated as a piercing pattern, this bullish candlestick must close above the midpoint of the body of the first bearish candle.

Interpreting the Pattern

When you observe the piercing candlestick pattern, it suggests that buyers have started to gain control of the market despite the recent downtrend. The significant gap down is indicative of initial selling pressure; however, the bullish candle closing above the 50% mark of the bearish candle's body is a strong signal that buying momentum is increasing. This closing position illustrates a shift in market sentiment, where buyers are overcoming the initial selling pressure and indicating that a reversal may be on the horizon.

For example, imagine that you are analysing the EUR/USD currency pair. You notice that after several weeks of consistently declining prices, a large red candlestick forms, closing at 1.1500. The following day, a bullish candlestick appears, opening at 1.1490 (thus creating a gap down) and then rallying to close at

1.1550. In this case, the second candlestick closes well above the midpoint of the earlier red candle, highlighting the strength of the bullish reversal.

Practical Application in Trading

When trading based on the piercing candlestick pattern, you should consider entering a long position following the confirmation provided by the bullish candlestick. A valid entry point might be placed just above the high of the second candlestick, which signals that upward momentum is likely to continue.

Using the earlier example of the EUR/USD pair, if the bullish candlestick's high is 1.1560, you might set a buy order at 1.1565. Additionally, it is essential to implement sound risk management strategies by placing a stop-loss order below the low of the bullish candlestick. This protective measure helps safeguard your position in case the market reverses unexpectedly.

Shooting Star (Bullish)

A shooting star candlestick is characterised by a distinct shape that emerges after a significant upward movement in price. This pattern typically forms following a bullish trend. To illustrate its formation, imagine a scenario where a currency pair opens at a certain price level and experiences a substantial rally throughout the trading session. During this upward movement, the price may rise significantly higher than the opening price, indicating strong buying activity.

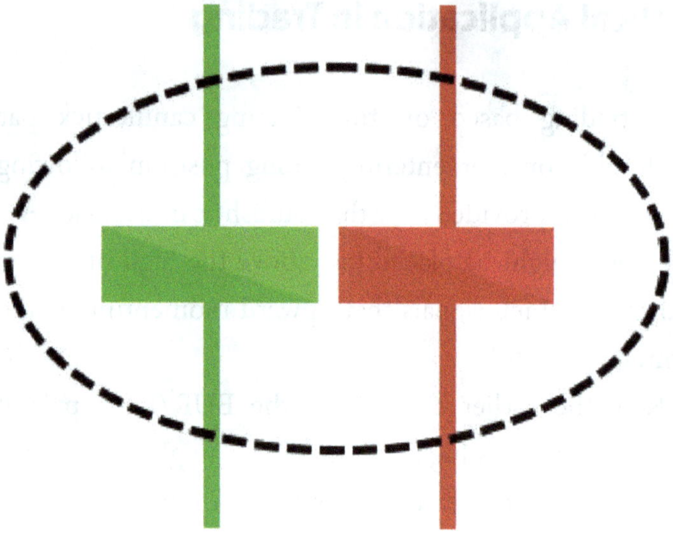

However, as the session progresses, the situation changes. Buyers start to lose their grip on the market, and selling pressure begins to take hold. Consequently, by the time the trading period concludes, the price closes near or below the original opening price.

Thus, the shooting star pattern is often described as having a small body located at the lower end of the price range and a long upper shadow, which signifies the peak price reached during that session. This long shadow demonstrates that although buyers pushed the price higher, they ultimately failed to maintain control, leading to a loss of momentum.

Interpreting the Shooting Star

The emergence of a shooting star pattern is a strong bearish signal, as it indicates that the buyers have been unable to sustain the earlier positive momentum. If you spot this pattern occurring at the top of an uptrend, it strongly suggests that sellers are preparing to enter the market, potentially leading to a downward price reversal.

For example, imagine analysing the USD/CHF currency pair. After a period of sustained upward movement, you notice the formation of a shooting star candlestick. The currency pair opens at 0.9400, climbs to a high of 0.9500 during the trading day, but closes back down near 0.9410. This formation signals to you that buyers are losing strength, and you might consider preparing for a potential sell opportunity.

Practical Application in Trading

When trading based on the shooting star pattern, it is prudent to look for confirmation. This could come in the form of subsequent bearish candlesticks that follow the shooting star, indicating that sellers have indeed taken control of the market. An ideal entry point for a sell order might be just below the low of the shooting star candlestick, which would indicate that the downward momentum is gaining strength.

Using the previous USD/CHF example, if the next candlestick confirms the bearish sentiment by closing lower than 0.9410, you would have a strong signal to place a sell order. Additionally, you should implement appropriate risk management strategies by placing a stop-loss order above the high of the shooting star to protect your position in case of an unexpected price movement.

Doji

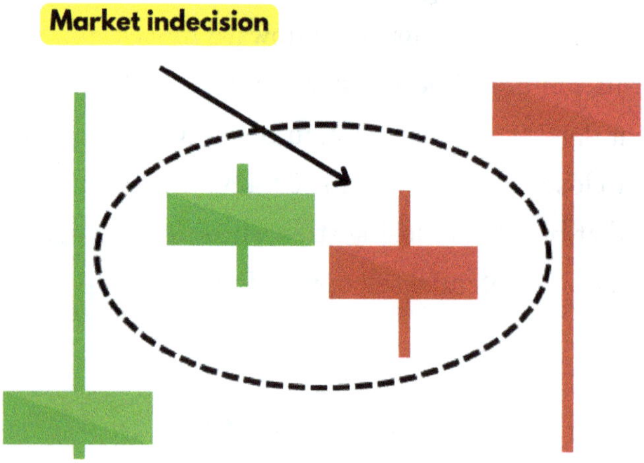

Doji candlesticks form when a stock's open and close are almost equal. The length of the upper and lower shadows can vary, and the resulting candlestick looks like a cross, an inverted cross, or a plus sign. A Doji indicates a sense of indecision between buyers and sellers.

Resistance and Support in Forex Trading

Resistance and support are important theories used in collaboration with trading in the Forex market. Methods of measurement, however, vary from trader to trader. To start with the basics, the zigzagging pattern is going upwards and this is known as the bull market. The resistance is the highest point before the market starts to recede, sometimes it will move upwards before it falls backwards. Conversely, as the Forex market starts moving back up, the point lowest reached is known as the support. As the market continues to change, support and resistance points continuously form.

The same can be observed when viewing downtrends in the market.

Forex Resistance and Support Plotting

It is important to note that the resistance and support figures are not precise. Where they are being tested by the market, they may not be accurate. In candlestick charts what is known as candlestick shadows are used to signify the market tests.

Understanding When the Resistance and Support Is Truly Broken

There is no definitive method for determining whether the support and resistance is broken, or even if there was a test.

One suggestion is that the Forex market can close after a certain level, then the resistance and support is broken. Generally though, this isn't true.

A method to prevent hasty actions is to consider resistance and support levels as different zones, instead of confirmed figures.

To help with the identification of these zones line charts give a better representation of the information, rather than candlesticks charts, when displaying the resistance and support. Candlestick charts are best for displaying the highs and lows visually, but line charts are a simpler method of just stating the closing price data. The vast visual array of data provided in a candlestick chart can be distracting and even misleading, and can influence more of a reflex response rather than a calculated one.

Line charts do not include reflex responses to graph resistance and support levels: only intentional actions are included. The chart below contains several valleys, which are where the resistance and support lines need to be plotted because they identify the price peaks and dips.

Bullish Harami

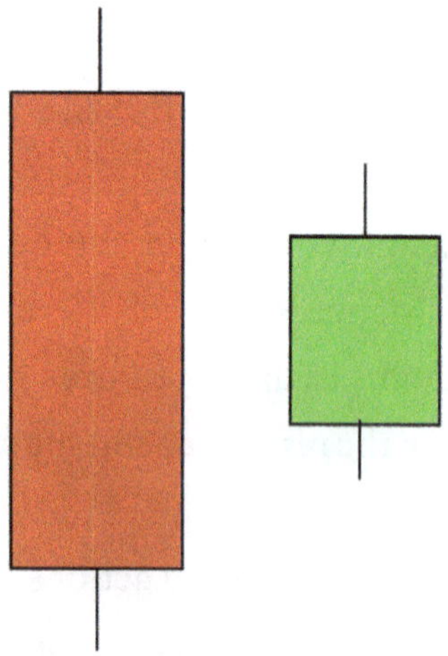

The bullish harami is a significant Japanese candlestick chart pattern that signals a potential reversal of a downtrend in the forex market. This pattern consists of two candlesticks: the first is a large bearish candle that continues the downtrend, and the second is a smaller bullish candle that appears within the body of the first candle.

Formation and Interpretation

The larger bearish candlestick indicates strong selling pressure, while the smaller bullish candle suggests a shift in momentum towards buying. For the pattern to be valid, the body of the small candle must be entirely contained within the body of the larger one. This containment reflects a weakening of the downtrend and hints at a possible bullish reversal.

For example, if you observe a bearish candle followed by a smaller bullish candle on the EUR/USD chart, this formation could indicate that selling pressure is lessening and that buyers may be starting to take control.

Practical Application

You should often wait for confirmation before acting on a harami signal. A subsequent bullish candle closing above the high of the small candle can validate the reversal. Additionally, incorporating other technical analysis tools, such as support levels or moving averages, can enhance the reliability of the bullish harami signal.

Three Outside Up

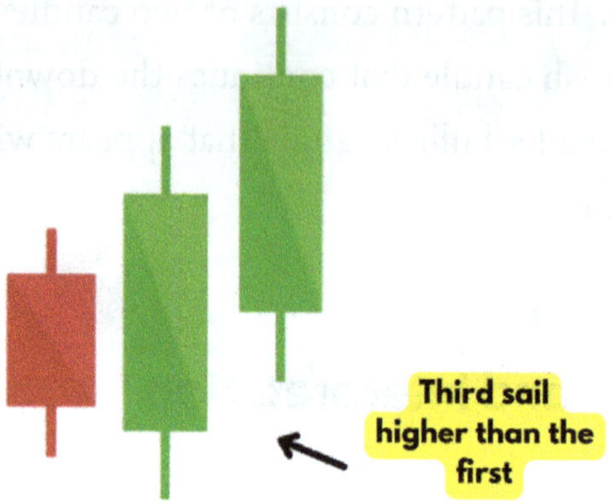

This pattern comprises three distinct candles. The first candle in the sequence is a short bearish candlestick, indicative of the prevailing downtrend. This candle reflects a period of selling pressure, typically characterized by a small body and a close near the low of the trading session.

The second candle is a larger bullish candlestick, which represents a significant shift in sentiment. This candle should completely envelop the body of the first bearish candle, demonstrating that buyers have begun to take control of the market. The fact that the bullish candlestick covers the entire body of the previous bearish candle is a key characteristic that signals a potential reversal.

The third candle further reinforces this bullish sign. It should be a long bullish candlestick that confirms the validity of the reversal pattern. This third candle's length indicates strong buying pressure and enthusiasm among market participants, affirming that the downward momentum has been successfully overcome.

Relationship to the Bullish Engulfing Pattern

The relationship between the first two candles in the three outside up pattern resembles that of the bullish engulfing candlestick pattern. In a bullish engulfing pattern, a smaller bearish candle is followed by a larger bullish candle that completely engulfs it. Similarly, in the three outside up pattern, the larger bullish candle envelops the smaller bearish candle, which is an essential aspect of confirming buyer strength.

Practical Application in Trading

When identifying this pattern on your price chart, look for it to form after a period of sustained bearish activity. The appearance of the three outside up patterns suggests that the selling pressure may have reached its limit, and a bullish reversal could be on the horizon.

Once you spot this formation, consider placing a buy order above the high of the third candlestick. This entry point indicates that the bullish movement is likely to continue, especially if it follows the confirmation provided by the long third candle.

Example Scenario

For example, suppose you are analysing the GBP/USD currency pair and notice the formation of a three outside up pattern after a downtrend. The first candlestick shows a small bearish body, followed by a larger bullish candle that completely covers the first. Then, the third candle emerges as a long bullish candlestick. If you decide to act on this pattern and set a buy order above the high of the third candle, you can potentially benefit from the anticipated upward movement in price.

On-Neck

The neckline pattern is composed of two distinct candlesticks. To begin with, a long bearish candlestick forms, which illustrates considerable selling pressure. This first candle signifies the strength of the downtrend by exhibiting a substantial body that reflects the dominance of sellers in the market.

Following the long bearish candle, a second candlestick appears, which is characterised by being bullish but opens with a gap down compared to the closing price of the previous candle. This gap down suggests that there is some buying interest; however, the bullish candle ultimately closes slightly below the low of the first long bearish candlestick. The presence of this weak bullish candle indicates the reluctance of buyers to push the price higher after the initial downtrend.

The formation of this pattern implies that, despite a temporary reversal, the overall market sentiment remains bearish. The inability of the bulls to sustain the upward movement reinforces the notion that sellers are still in control.

Importance of Confirmation

For the neckline pattern to serve as a reliable signal for a continuation of the downtrend, it is crucial to seek confirmation from a third candlestick. This confirmation typically comes in the form of a subsequent bearish candle that closes lower than the second bullish candle. When you observe this third bearish candlestick following the formation of the neckline pattern, it solidifies the expectation that the downtrend will continue.

Practical Application in Trading

When identifying the neckline pattern on your trading charts, particularly in the context of a preceding downtrend, it is essential to be mindful of the specific characteristics of the candlesticks involved. Once you spot the long bearish candle followed by the weaker bullish candle with a gap down, it indicates potential selling opportunities.

For example, if you are analysing the USD/JPY currency pair and you observe the formation of the neckline pattern after a downtrend, your strategy might involve placing a sell order just below the low of the second bullish candle. This approach takes advantage of the expected continuation of the downtrend.

Tweezer Button

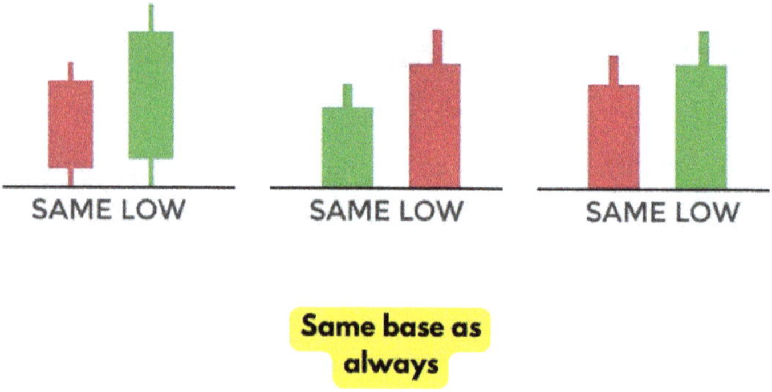

The tweezer bottom candlestick pattern is a significant bullish reversal signal in the world of forex trading. This pattern typically appears at the conclusion of a bearish trend, suggesting that the market sentiment may be shifting from bearish to bullish. By recognising this pattern, you can make more informed trading decisions that align with potential upward movements in the market.

Formation of the Tweezer Bottom Pattern

The tweezer bottom consists of two distinct candlesticks that share a common feature: both candles have the same price bottom, indicating a strong level of support. The first candle in the pattern is a bearish candlestick, which reflects continuing selling pressure and likely represents the prevailing downtrend. Following this bearish candle, the second candle is bullish, suggesting that buyers are beginning to enter the market.

An essential aspect of the tweezer bottom is that the colour of the candles does not impact the validity of the pattern; what matters is that both candles reach the same low price point. Therefore, whether the first candle is red (bearish) and the second candle is green (bullish) or vice versa, the important factor is the alignment of their lows. The signals do not have to be consecutive; this means that the two candles forming the tweezer bottom pattern can occur with other price action in between them, further broadening the contexts in which this pattern can be identified.

Interpretation and Significance

When you encounter the tweezer bottom pattern at the end of a bearish trend on a forex chart, it suggests that the downtrend may be losing momentum and that a reversal could be imminent. The equal lows formed by the two candles signal strong buying support at that price level, indicating that buyers are willing to step in and prevent the price from falling further.

For example, if you are analysing the EUR/USD currency pair and observe a bearish trend followed by a bearish candle closing at a certain low, then the next candle is bullish and also closes at that same low, you have identified a tweezer bottom.

This formation implies that the market is finding support at that price level, and you might consider this an indication to look for potential buying opportunities.

Triple Top

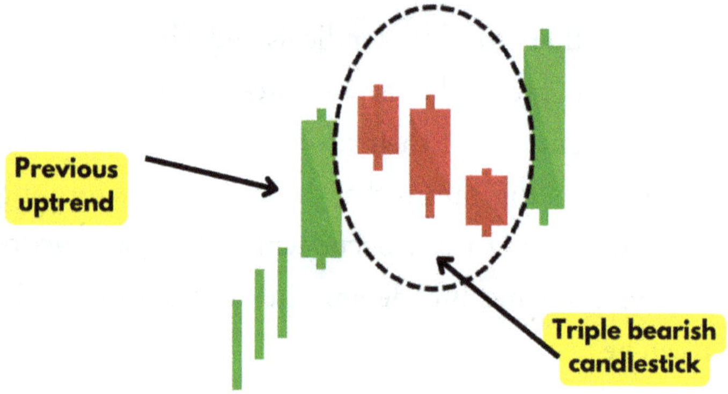

Contrary to what its name might suggest, the triple top is not a bearish reversal pattern – instead, it serves as a bullish continuation pattern, indicating that a price break is likely to occur in a previously established upward trend.

Formation of the Triple Top Pattern

The triple top pattern is characterised by a specific arrangement of five candlesticks. The formation begins with two large bullish candlesticks that demonstrate strong upward momentum, reflecting significant buying interest in the market. These bullish candles are then followed by three smaller-bodied bearish candlesticks. These bearish candles represent temporary pullbacks that occur after the bullish movement, as profit-taking may take place among traders looking to secure gains.

The key feature of this pattern is that the three bearish candlesticks create new lows, but crucially, these lows are contained within the body of the first large bullish candlestick. This configuration illustrates that while there is selling pressure evident in the market, it is ultimately unable to break below the territory established by the initial bullish movement.

Interpreting the Pattern

The presence of the triple top pattern following a preceding uptrend can signal a potential break rather than a reversal. Traders interpret this formation as an indication that the buying momentum is still very much intact despite the pullbacks represented by the bearish candles. The market is essentially consolidating before resuming its upward trend, as the repeated challenges to the previous high points reinforce the strength of the bullish sentiment.

For example, imagine you are examining the USD/JPY currency pair on your trading chart. After a sustained period of growth, you observe two large bullish candlesticks that push the price higher, followed by three smaller bearish candles that descend slightly but remain contained within the first bullish candle's body. This observation suggests to you that the market is engaged in a consolidation phase and that further upward movement is imminent.

Moving onto the bullish candlestick signals

Resistance and Support in the Forex Market:

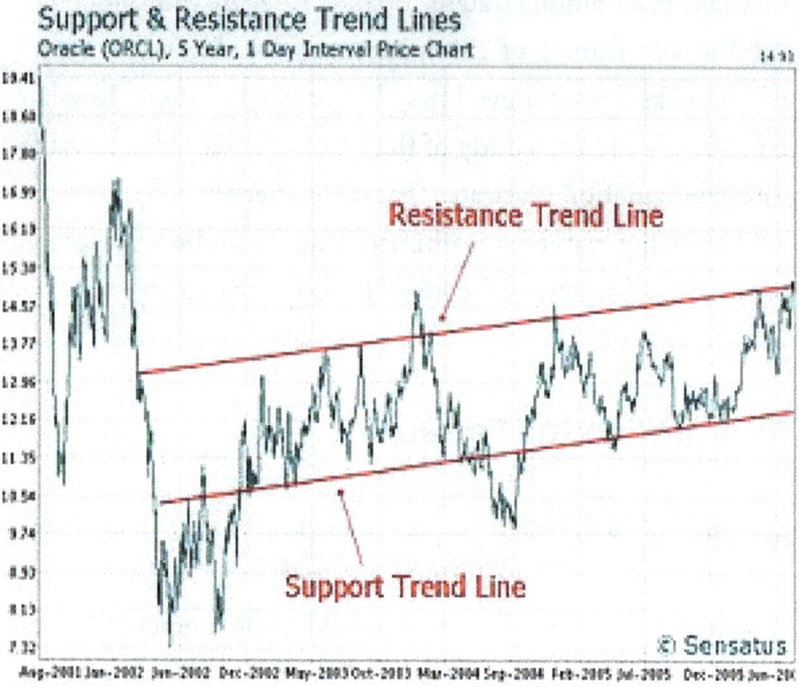

If a price has the opportunity to pass through a resistance, it may convert into a support.

If a price tests the resistance or support levels they might increase in strength.

If a strong support or resistance is broken, the follow-through move will be proportionately strong also.

Traders require experience to identify opportunities through analysis of resistance and support levels.

The following section will cover trend lines and how these can be used to commence trading with the use of diagonal resistance and support lines.

Trend Lines

Trend lines are a popular method of technical analysis in the Forex market. Unfortunately, although they are common, they are also not used to their full potential.

Trend lines contain the same information as other types of charts but need a greater level of accuracy to be useful. Issues arise when traders attempt to manipulate the lines to match the market when, in actual fact, they should do the complete opposite. Some simply don't know how to draw the trend lines at all.

To begin with the fundamentals of trend lines, the support areas are easily spotted and the uptrend line needs to be plotted at the bottom. The opposite contains the resistance areas and the trend line, drawn at the top, plots the peaks.

Drawing the Trend Lines

Trend lines are easily plotted in the Forex market. Two major tops or bottoms must be identified, and then joined together.

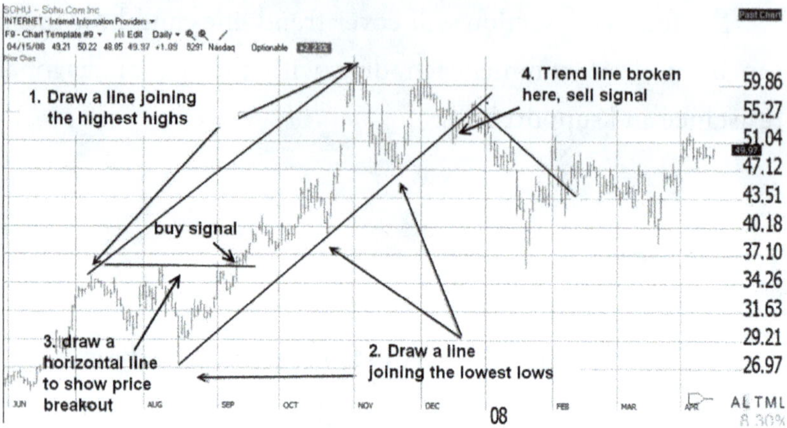

That's it! The following will expand on this.

The Different Trend Types

There are three main types of trend lines:

Higher lows – the uptrend

Lower highs – the downtrend

Ranging – sideways trends

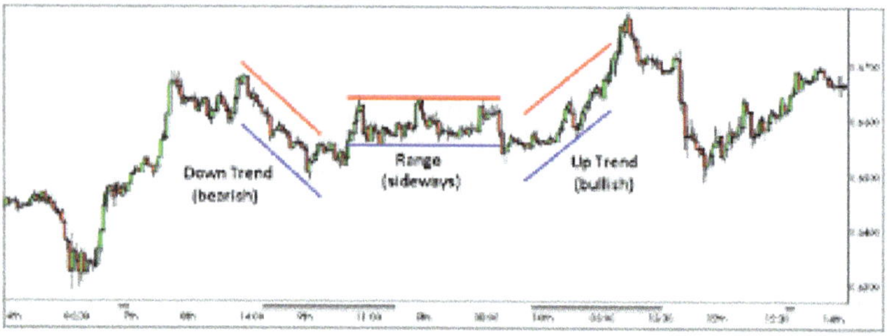

Important Information to Consider When Using Forex Trend Lines

It is possible to plot a trend line with only two bottoms or tops, but three are necessary to corroborate the line.

The steeper the trend line, the less dependable it becomes – to the point that it may break altogether once it reaches a certain height.

As with horizontal testing, testing a trend line increases its strength.

Never make a trend line try to fit in with the market; if you force it, then it won't be valid to use. Forcing a trend line to conform with the market causes it to become void and unusable.

Channels

The theory of the trend line is enhanced with the addition of a channel. This occurs when a parallel line is added to the angle that the downtrend or uptrend follows. A channel, in this case, is not a television channel, but that doesn't mean that it can't be exciting! Channels are technical tools that are useful for identifying locations that may be suitable for buying and selling. Resistance or support areas can appear at the bottom and top of a channel. Channels are simple to draw – just draw a line parallel to the uptrend line and then move the line to make sure that it is able to touch the final peak on the chart. This needs to be done while the trend line is being drawn. In contrast, to draw a descending channel, the downtrend line, the opposite must be done, ensuring that the line touches the final valley on the chart.

It is important that, again, the trend line is completed at the same time. The selling and buying areas are located when prices reach either the lower trend line for buying, or the top trend line for selling.

The Different Channel Types

There are three distinct types of channel:

Higher highs and higher lows – known as an ascending channel;

Lower highs and lower lows – known as a descending channel;

Ranging – known as a horizontal channel.

Things Not to Forget When Drawing Your Trend Lines

When making a channel, ensure that the trend lines stay parallel.

In the majority of the examples, the sell zone will appear at the top of the channel and the buy zone will appear at the bottom.

Similar to trends, channels shouldn't be forced. Disastrous trading decisions are made when the channel's boundaries are sloping at each end.

Trading with Resistance and Support

With the knowledge learned regarding resistance and support, it becomes easier to see how the technical tools are relevant for trading in the Forex market. To clarify the best method of trading using the levels of resistance and support, these two concepts have been divided into two categories, called the break and the bounce.

The Bounce

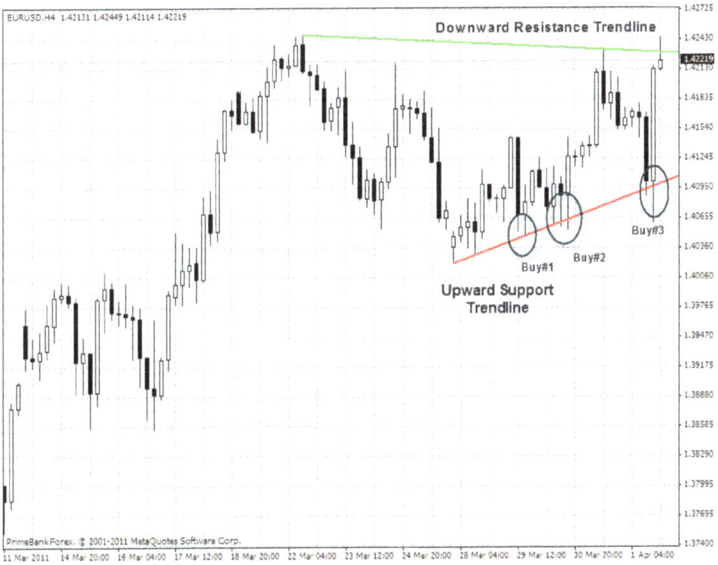

A bounce is an activity carried out in anticipation of the commencement of trading in the resistance and support levels. Traders will often wait for a trade to occur, the knowledge of which they have gleaned from the orders that have been set due to the levels of resistance and support. This approach is occasionally successful, but is based on the theory that the level is always going to hold and that the price will never arrive. A common assumption would be that a good idea would be to enter the market with an entry order exactly positioned on the line in order to obtain the best price in the market. With a bounce, however, holding the levels needs to be confirmed and the probabilities need to be in your favour. In contrast to straightforward buying or selling when the options are favourable, a bounce needs to appear before any action is taken. If this is not done there is the risk of a price crash through the levels occurring. In trading, this can be described as trying to catch a fast-falling knife: the results can be a disaster.

In a perfect trading market, the resistance and support levels would maintain an infinite steady position. The optimum Forex market would earn traders millions by diving into the market immediately when the prices reached the major levels in resistance and support. In reality, however, this does not happen and traders must constantly negotiate levels that regularly break.

Just as a trader must recognise when to bounce, they must also know what to do when the resistance and support levels break.

Traders have the option of taking an aggressive or a passive position when trading on the Forex market breaks.

Aggressive

One of the simplest methods to deal with breakouts in the Forex market is to buy or sell as soon as the price has gone through the resistance or support zones. It is vital, however, not to act in haste and to ensure that the price has passed through the levels with certainty, not hesitancy, before a position is taken.

The price must move confidently through the resistance and support before a trader enters the market.

Conservative

Consider the example of a trader deciding to play the waiting game with the exchange of two currencies in the anticipation that they will shortly increase once they bounce off the support level. However, before that occurs, the bounce level breaks and the trader suffers heavy losses because they took an incorrect position.

The trader then has two options: either get out and give up; or hold on to the long-term approach with the hope that the prices will rise at a later date.

This "hold" position would be more in line with a conservative method of trading. This is where a trader takes the opposite side of trade when they go to close their position. If the trader is close to a position on the two currencies near the break-even point, that amount will have to be shortened to the exchange rates between the two currencies.

The price will once again fall when the support levels are broken and when one side sells or liquidates to a sufficient level.

Patience is the best characteristic to have to most benefit from this type of event. Regardless of whether it is the support level or the resistance level that is broken, patience is needed to hold until the price makes a pullback, and then the trader can enter the market once the price begins to bounce.

Unfortunately, due to the fickle nature of the Forex market, this result cannot be assured every time.

Retesting does not always occur on resistance and support levels that are broken. Unfortunately, once a price has set off in a certain direction it does not pause for traders to catch up. Don't rely on expectations: make use of stop-loss orders as they can provide a barrier to heavy losses due to holding on for too long.

A Summary of Resistance and Support Trading in Forex

The resistance is the highest point reached, prior to a downward movement.

The support is the opposite; it is the lowest valley reached before the market started going up.

Numbers used in horizontal levels of resistance and support are not tangible.

To differentiate between a false or true breakout, consider resistance and support as different zones.

Information read from a line chart can be easier to analyse than that displayed on a candlestick chart.

If a price has the opportunity to pass through resistance levels it can sometimes convert into support levels. The opposite can also be true, where broken levels of support can convert into a resistance level.

Trend Lines

For ease of identification, a downtrend goes at the top of a resistance area and an uptrend goes at the bottom of a support area.

The three different kinds of trends are:

Higher lows – uptrends

Lower highs – downtrends

Ranging – sideways trends

Channels

To create an ascending channel, a parallel line must be plotted to match the angle of a line that displays the uptrend and then needs to be moved to touch the final peak on the chart. To create a descending channel a parallel line must be drawn to match the angle of a line that shows the downtrend and then needs to be moved to touch the final valley on the chart:

Higher highs and higher lows is an ascending channel;

Lower highs and lower lows is a descending channel;

Ranging is a horizontal channel.

Trading can be divided into the resistance and support levels with two distinctive methods: the break; and the bounce. With the bounce method, traders need to find guarantees that the two levels will hold and that the events will prove beneficial to themselves.

Prior to commencing buying and selling, traders must wait for the bounce. This is to avoid the risk of trading when the price can still crash through the levels. The break method can be managed either conservatively or aggressively.

Trading aggressively consists of making a decision and entering the market when there is no resistance or as the price moves through the resistance or support zones. Conservative trading means waiting until the price has begun its pullback towards either the resistance or support level that has been broken, moving only when the price has finished bouncing.

Proficiency in identifying each type is necessary for trading in the Forex market.

For each chart you need to identify and run through:

- Number of Bars
- Bullish or Bearish?

What does it look like?

- Spinning Top
- Neutral
- Doji
- Neutral
- Shooting Star

A Summary of the Japanese Candlestick Charts

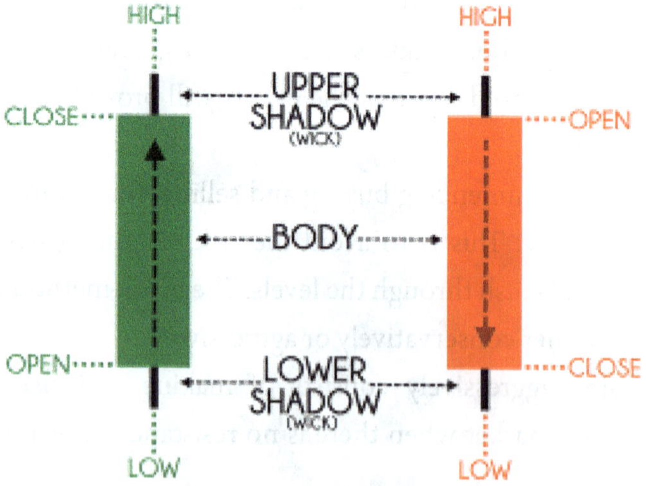

The body, or the real body, is the section of the candlestick that is filled or hollowed.

The shadows are the lines that are drawn above and below the main body of the candlestick and are used to show the high and low range.

The shadow at the top displays the high.

The shadow at the bottom depicts the law. The long part of the candle's body depicts the strength of the buying and selling, and the length of the body signifying the strength of the pressure to buy or sell. Short bodies mean very little buying or selling activities. To simplify things, traders label sellers as 'bears' and buyers 'bulls'. The shadows at the top can give information on the session high and the shadows at the bottom can show the session low details. There are various patterns found in Japanese candlestick charts. They can be grouped together by the number of bars needed to formulate their patterns. The three candlestick pattern formations are the triple, the dual and the single designs.

Number of Bars in a Japanese Candlestick Pattern:

Single
Dojis, Marubozu, Hanging Man, Inverted Hammer, Shooting Star, Spinning Tops

Double
Tweezer Tops and Bottoms, Bullish and Bearish Engulfing

Triple
Three Black Crows and Three White Soldiers, Morning and Evening Stars, Three Inside Up and Down

For the best results it is advised that the candlestick charts and analysis is used alongside the resistance and support levels.

Even if all of the evidence on the candlesticks state that there will be a continuation or reversal, this should not be taken as a guarantee. This information needs to be taken into consideration in conjunction with price action and the present state of the market.

As we have seen by now the Forex market can be extremely volatile!

Understanding How to Use Fibonacci Trading

Trading cannot be carried out without some use of Fibonacci ratios. These include huge amounts of data, but for the present, the two main theories expanded on here are extension and retracement.

Fibonacci trading and ratios are named after Leonardo Fibonacci, an Italian-born mathematician.

The ratios that he discovered use a number series that can calculate the proportions of all of the natural things that can be found in our universe.

The ratios comprise the following series of numbers: 0, 1, 1, 2, 3, 5, 8, 13, 21, 34, 55, 89, 144, etc.

The series is created by starting with 0, then adding 1. These are added together to get the third number in the series, 1. The second and the third numbers are added, 2, and then the third and fourth, 3, and so on to infinity.

In this progression of numbers, the ratio of a number to its subsequent number is 0.618. For example, take 34 and divide it by 55 and the result is 0.618.

Using every second number is different, however, with a result of 0.382. For example, again take 34 and divide it by 89 and the result is 0.382. This is the core premise of the Fibonacci series.

These calculated ratios are known as the 'golden mean'. Although the sequences are necessary, the important information is the ratios – only a few of which are needed to be recognised and understood.

Retracement Levels
0.236, 0.382, 0.500, 0.618, 0.764

Extension Levels
0, 0.382, 0.618, 1.000, 1.382, 1.618

A trader does not need to have the ability to calculate these sequences themselves. There is trading software available for charting that will include the ability to compute this, included below. Although this document will carry out all the calculations, it is necessary to understand where the figures are coming from.

The retracement levels from Fibonacci are used by traders to find resistance and support areas. These normally behave as they are supposed to and so traders can be confident knowing when to buy or sell, or to enter trades or place stops. The extension levels, on the other hand, can be used as levels to make profits.

This tool often reaches its potential and traders use it to observe levels to put in orders and gain profits. Regardless of the software used, the extension levels and retracement levels information will be pre-programmed. This is not enough to obtain the full picture, however; and to obtain the full picture the levels need to be inserted into the charts and the Swing Low points and the Swing High points need to be identified.

A Swing high is when a candlestick chart has a double lower high, or more, on the right and left. A Swing low is when a candlestick chart has a double higher low, or more, on the right and left.

A further explanation of retracements and extensions will come later in this book, along with how best to use the Fibonacci tool to make money.

The Fibonacci tool shows maximum benefits when it is trending in the market.

https://www.investing.com/tools/fibonacci-calculator

The most common theory is that if the Forex market looks to be trending down, then traders should sell a retracement at the level of Fibonacci resistance, and when it is trending up, traders should buy a retracement at the level of Fibonacci support.

How to Locate the Retracement Levels

To identify the retracement levels first locate the recent major Swing lows or Swing highs. The swing highs will then need to be pulled over to the Swing lows while checking the downtrends.

To locate the uptrends, the same process must be carried out, just in reverse – the Swing lows need to be pulled over to the most recent Swing highs.

The Way to Enter a Trade Using Retracement

Once an understanding of retracement levels has been achieved, this can be utilised in the Forex market.

The expectation would be that the downtrend would experience resistance at the Fibonacci level because of the chance that traders will seize the opportunity of the downtrend to earn profits by selling, if the price retracts from the Swing low.

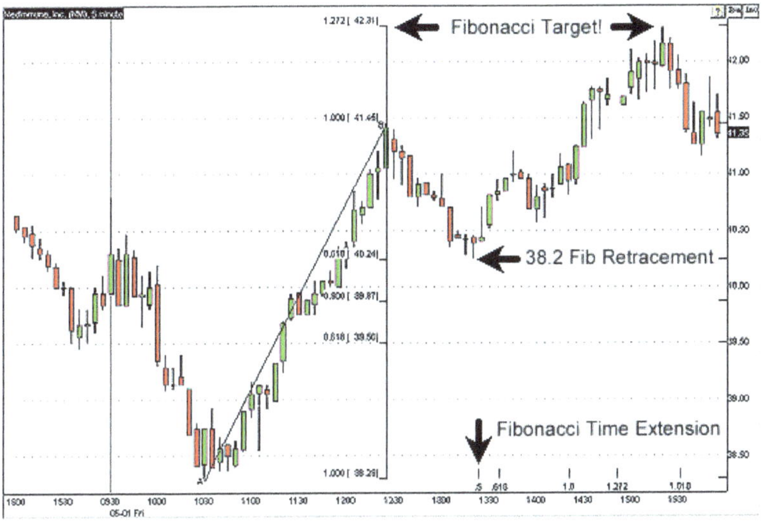

The extensive use of the Fibonacci software has led to the outlook levels for resistance and support are usually achieved. It must be highlighted that there is never a certainty that the price will bounce. This will be explained in greater depth later, but the areas highlighted are not definite, but rather areas worth noting, or kill zones.

Although the theory is easy, the Fibonacci software is not. Traders need to be aware of this. If everything was easy, traders would place their orders depending on the levels of Fibonacci's retracement, and the Forex market would continuously trend.

The following will explain what happens when the retracement levels fail.

It has already been explained that all levels of resistance and support can be broken. Fibonacci levels can experience this also, which is obvious if remembered that they can be used to find the resistance and support levels.

It is possible that the retracement levels will break. As with the majority of things in the Forex market, they are not completely dependable.

A trader identifies a downtrend in a pair and reckons on locating the optimum entry with use of the retracement tool.

The trader observes the Fibonacci hold and commits to his position.

Expecting huge profits, he shorts the market.

He had forgotten that there are no guarantees with Fibonacci retracements!

If this order had been completed, heavy losses would have been incurred.

Let us examine what went wrong.

The market concentrated on the Swing high because the Swing low appeared at the very bottom of the downtrend.

As with all of the other trading tools and theories previously discussed, it is important to note that the Fibonacci retracement can only give suggestions for financial success, but no guarantees.

It is impossible to forecast whether the price will hold or reverse back to the previous position.

The money markets are completely unpredictable. The price may hold, or it could reach much higher and then just completely change and go backwards. It doesn't take retracement levels into account at all.

Even though an uptrend made use of a temporary resistance or support, this does not ensure that it will continue on. It could simply ignore any recent Swing lows or Swing highs.

Another issue with the Fibonacci retracement is that it does not identify which are the optimum Swing highs and Swing lows to use.

Each trader will consider the charts differently, depending on their biases or the time frames shown. This means that there will not be a general consensus on where the points should be located.

The truth of the matter is that there is no definitive method for choosing the points: it is simply guesswork.

This is why the retracement tools are not a stand-alone method and should be used in conjunction with various other tools. This increases traders' chances of expanding their skill and experience levels and of succeeding in business.

The use of retracement tools in collaboration with other financial tools, including candlesticks.

Although the retracement tool is open to interpretation it can certainly be used in specific ways that will increase the odds in your favour.

Again, to clarify, the retracement software should never be completely relied upon and should be used in conjunction with other tools.

Even the most effective, proficient tools need support, which is why it is best to use the Fibonacci tool with some of the other technical tools. With the previous knowledge gained, several strong trades will now be examined.

It's time to make money!

Using Resistance and Support with the Fibonacci Tool

Retracement Tool

The main strength of the Fibonacci tool is how it can identify possible resistance and support levels, and then examine them to determine if the levels equal the retracement levels. The chance of a price bouncing can be increased when the resistance and support levels are retracement levels and if this is joined with areas that are heavily observed by many traders.

Using Resistance and Support with Retracement

A current uptrend with many green candlesticks is displayed on the chart. This would make traders inclined to enter into trading.

When all of the information is input, the only question left to answer is 'where is the best place to enter?'.

Retracing the steps in the chart it's easy to see the price with its prior promising level of resistance. This is also in line with the retracement level. Therefore, there is a chance that it could become a support, seeing as it had previously been broken, suggesting that it would be a perfect buying place.

Traders mainly concentrate on those areas of promise to buy or sell in, in particular previous levels of resistance and support.

However, as the Fibonacci retracement levels are so reputable, chances are that many other traders will be doing the same thing.

The quantity of orders will more than likely be greater than those at set price levels because of the amount of traders scrutinising the levels of resistance and support.

There is no guarantee with this, just as there is no definite way of knowing whether the price will bounce or not. It will, however, boost trading confidence, along with the increased strength experienced with the large number of traders deciding to enter the market.

Trading and the Forex market are based on chance, with the greater the chance of a trade the greater the chance that it will be profitable.

Using Trade Lines and Retracement Together

Trade lines and retracement tools are strong tools to use together for the analysis of trade lines. A trending market is useful for retracement and so using the two together is very beneficial. Remembering that traders use retracement levels to trade when a pair is experiencing either an uptrend or a downtrend, then it is reasonable to situate lines where the trend is similar to the retracement levels.

If a more specific entry price is required, then it's beneficial to obtain further information from the retracement tool, the Swing high, having first touched the trend line.

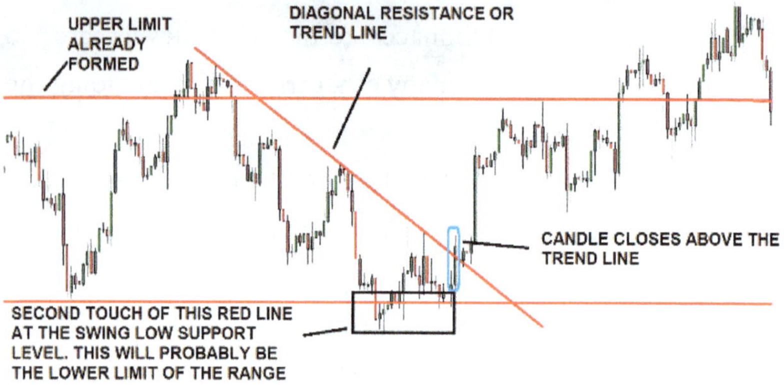

Even when the decision is taken to enter the market during a trend line retest, it is worth using the retracement tools to evaluate the market. This is because if a horizontal and diagonal level of resistance or support appears, chances are that there are many more traders also watching the levels.

It is very important to remember that when you are examining the drawing your approach is a personal one, and that what you interpret from the information will be different from everyone else.

Even when you are certain that a trend is there, each trader will draw different lines.

A profit is more likely when there is a long trend, so this is what to watch out for on the charts.

Merging the resistance levels and support with the retracement levels will create profitable trading strategies. Adding the trade lines is also necessary.

Retracement

Traders need to investigate whether there is enough of a chance in the downtrend to commit to a move. Fibonacci's retracement tool helps to show the best time to short and earn profits is when the doji first appears.

Again a doji is a name for a session in which the candlestick for a security has an open and close that are virtually equal and are often components in patterns.

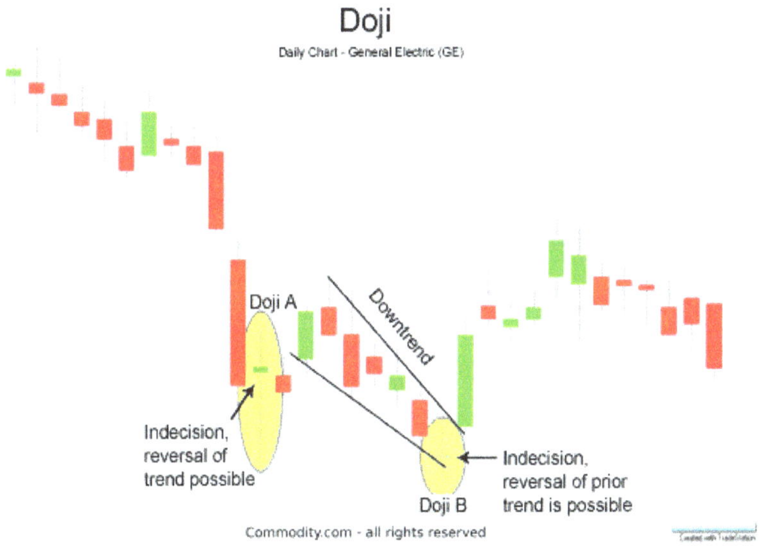

The Fibonacci candlesticks are extremely useful for identifying whether the retracement is going to hold or not. If multiple traders place orders at the retracement level, this may cause the retracement level to stall, and it is possible that support or resistance could be recognised at the price if this is noticed.

Limit orders are unnecessary on the retracement level if the Fibonacci candlesticks are being used. There is a degree of uncertainty regarding whether the levels will hold because the levels are not definite, but rather zones.

An understanding of the workings of candlestick chart formations is very useful in this situation.

The best way of identifying whether an order should be placed is to see if a Fibonacci candlestick occurs either just below or just above a retracement level.

If it does, this is a validation that a level is likely to hold, and a trade can occur with the use of the market price.

Understand the Best Time to Take Profits Using the Fibonacci Extensions

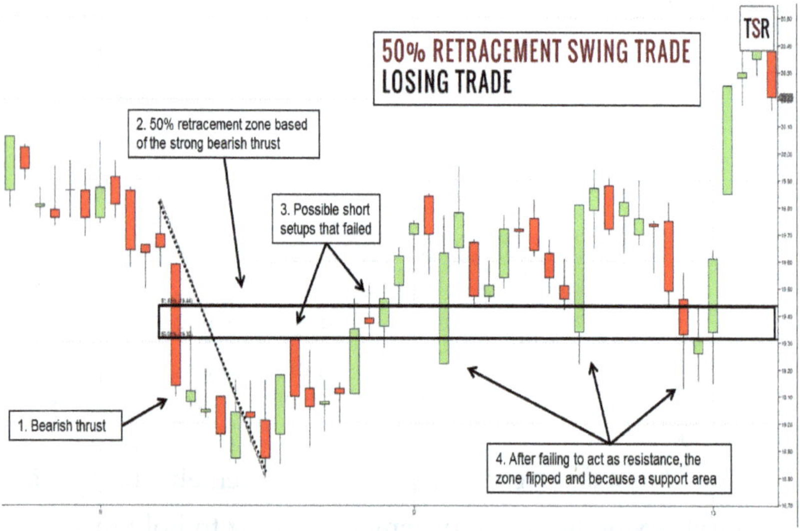

Finding targets can also be done through the Fibonacci ratios. Remember that a trader can always get out of a trade if there is any doubt. Using an uptrend as an example, remember that the majority of uptrends are for making long trades to earn profits, using the price extension level. From there it is very quick and easy to find out the extension levels.

First, the major Swing low needs to be chosen and then pulled across the most recent Swing high. Following this, a retracement level can be chosen.

This will display the price and the ratio of the extension levels.

The extension tool can now be used to identify when to take off the profits.

It is probable that more traders were watching the swing levels for the same purpose. This is the reason that the levels could be considered as support. Although not certain as the extension levels deliver short-lived resistance or support for the price, altering positions can manage risk when obtaining profits.

The main issue here is that it is impossible to identify the correct extension that will provide resistance.

Neither resistance nor support were or weren't found anywhere on the levels. When deciding on the levels, the starting Swing low also needs to be determined. There is a choice available between the lowest Swing low among the last 30 bars or the one used previously. The extension tools can be used depending on preferences and it's up to you to determine when the trend will end. Later on, how to determine a brand's strength will be explained, but stop loss placement must be clarified first.

Managing Risk by Placing Stops with Fibonacci

Knowing where to put a stop loss is as important as recognizing the optimum time to enter a trade or the best time to seize profits.

A trader shouldn't enter into a trade just because the Fibonacci levels indicate that it is a good time without knowing where to get out. This would be a disaster for their account.

The following will explain how to use Fibonacci levels in parallel to setting stops. The rationale for each method for setting stops will also be discussed.

Directly after the Fibonacci level is the best location for the first stop.

If placing discontinues using this method then the best entry is needed, which could trigger problems.

To demonstrate your confidence in your forecasting for the resistance or support areas holding then you should put a stop following the next retracement level on the chart.

Unfortunately, as already discussed, drawing tools are not an infallible system.

There is always the risk that the market will rocket up, hit your stop, and then advance towards you. That would be annoying.

As with all trading, there is no assurance that this will occur, and none that it won't several times all together. It is vital to remember to permit successes to keep moving along the trend, and to straight away halt those that don't. These stop placement methods are best matched to intraday and short-term trades.

It is more of a guarantee to place stops just after the most recent Swing low or high.

If this is done, there will be more room to manoeuvre your trade and will allow the Forex market more time to amend itself in your favour.

You can see a current trend reversal from the price increasing over the Swing low or high. However, at this stage the idea is nullified and it's all over.

A larger stop loss is more appropriate for long-term swing-type trades. The scaling method is also useful and so this will be explained later on.

A larger stop always necessitates an alteration in the position size.

In particular, if choosing to enter a trade based on an early Fibonacci level, you could incur major losses if you used an unaltered position size.

If you do this, and have a wider stop that doesn't equate to the prospective gain, there is not going to be much of a ratio of risk and reward.

Which way Is the Best?

The best method for choosing a stop loss for your present trade is to inspect the environment. This is identical to the use of the retracement tool to identify an entry in union with the trend line, candlesticks, and resistance and support.

It is important not to place all of your reliance on the Fibonacci resistance and support levels though, when placing your stop loss.

Again, it must be stressed, there are no guarantees when placing the stop loss. If you use multiple tools, however, it gives you a greater chance of success. This can raise the risk and reward ratios, you could find a better exit point and you will have more breathing room for your trade.

A Summary of Trading with Fibonacci

The most important retracement levels are 23.6%, 38.2%, 50.0%, 61.8% and 76.4%. The levels, 38.2%, 50.0%, and 61.8%, would seem to have a definite weight and are commonly used in default settings in the majority of Forex trading chart software.

Retracement levels are normally thought to be areas of possible resistance and support. This is often found to be true due to the large number of traders who observe them.

The main extension levels are 38.2%, 50.0%, 61.8%, 100%, 138.2% and 161.8%.

Forex traders commonly make use of extension levels as potential areas of resistance and support to establish profit targets. These are often found to be true as traders observe these so as to put in orders and earn profits.

In order to be able to utilise the Fibonacci levels to the charts, the Swing high and low points need to be located.

A Swing high candlestick can be recognised by the two or more lower highs located to its left and right.

A Swing low candlestick can be recognised by the two or more higher lows on either side of it to the right and left.

Using Fibonacci tools and a greater number of trend lines, candlestick patterns, and resistance and support levels give a better chance of successful trading and spotting stop loss locations and entry.

Understanding Moving Averages

The use of moving averages is beneficial for smoothing price action over a certain period of time. This theory relates to how an average closing currency of the price of a pair is used over specific periods. The following is how you would expect to see this displayed on a chart:

As with all of the other indicators, this is useful for calculating future prices. If the slope that the moving average creates can be seen, this will provide a better gauge of the direction of the market price.

In summary, a moving average is useful for smoothing out the price action.

The degree of smoothness is reliant on the type of moving average you use.

The smoothness of the moving average dictates the reaction time of the price movement: the smoother it is, the slower the response time.

A choppy moving average is used for rapid reactions.

The smoother the moving average, the longer the period to take the closing price average from.

We will now see how to apply this to actual trading.

The two primary moving averages are: simple; and exponential.

The pros and cons of each will be discussed and methods of calculating them will also be included.

Once this has been explained, we will continue on to the methods in which moving averages can be used and how they can be applied to your trading strategy.

You will be proficient in averages by the end of this.

First you will be introduced to simple moving averages (SMA), which are the easiest moving averages in the Forex market. To calculate these, you need to take the closing prices of a specific period, then the number of periods, and divide this second figure into the first.

As we continue on this will become clearer.

How the Simple Moving Average Is Calculated

$SMA = (P[1] + P[2] + P[3] + \ldots P[N]) \div N$

Where: N is the number of periods in the SMA

P[N] is the price being averaged (usually the closing price)

A tool to use is available at StockCharts.com

Closer examination shows that the calculations are not that difficult to carry out. Take an SMA for a 5-period using a 1-hour chart, for example, and just add 5 hours' worth of closing prices, and divide that by 5. The result would be the average of the closing prices over a 5-hour period. So, a moving average can be obtained by lining up all of the average prices together.

If a 10-minute chart was used, then the 5-period SMA would be calculated by adding the prior minutes of closing time and dividing the result by 5.

In a 30-minute chart, the 150 prior minutes of closing prices need to be added, and divided by 5 to calculate a 5-period SMA.

Thankfully, most software programs will carry out the calculations, but knowing the background is always good when using these tools to gain a deeper understanding.

Once the mechanics of indicators are understood, care must be taken to know how to adapt a strategy to keep pace with any environmental changes. As with many of the indicators available, moving averages have a delay.

Moving averages give an outline of the future course of price action in the short-term. They demonstrate the route taken recently as moving averages are calculated in the average price history.

The SMA is useful for gauging the overall present market opinion at that time.

The SMA demonstrates a wider view of the market so it gives a better indication of the direction prices may go in the future. SMAs are useful for indicating if a pair is ranging, trending down, or trending up.

Unfortunately, SMAs are influenced by spikes, which causes an issue as this can give false readings. Even though nothing actually changed, the charts could show a trend starting.

There is another type of moving average that avoids this issue, which will be covered as follows, along with the actual problem.

Understanding the Exponential Moving Average

As mentioned previously, SMAs can sometimes be influenced by market spikes.

Check out the example below:

First, we need to use a EUR/USD to plot an SMA over a 5-period.

The closing prices over the 5 days are:

Day 1: 1.3172

Day 2: 1.3231

Day 3: 1.3164

Day 4: 1.3186

Day 5: 1.3293

We simply need to add these up and divide by 5 to calculate the SMA of 1.3209.

If, however, an event occurred on Day 2 (some breaking news bulletin) that changed the closing price of EUR/USD to 1.3000 instead, the details below show how this dramatically alters the 5-period SMA.

Day 1: 1.3172

Day 2: 1.3000

Day 3: 1.3164

Day 4: 1.3186

Day 5: 1.3293

The SMA would then be achieved by adding the 5 closing prices and dividing them by 5, which is 1.3163.

Even though what happened on Day 2 was just a glitch, the chart information now suggests that the price of the market was dropping because the SMA was considerably lower.

Although, overall, the SMA is a useful tool, it is sometimes considered too simplistic and not inclusive of any other factors.

There is a better tool that can spot and abolish spikes so that the readings don't give an inaccurate picture of the market situation.

This tool is the exponential moving average, or EMA, and it is the second moving average. The most recent periods receive greater credibility when this is used. If the same chart as above was used but an EMA applied instead for analysis, additional weight would have been given to the third, fourth, and fifth day.

If this had been done then the second day spike would not have had as great an effect as with the SMA, due to the days after it receives extra weight. Using an EMA is better because of the additional weight placed on the most recent days and the most recent behaviour of other traders.

Using a Simple Moving Average and Exponential Moving Average Together

The EMA displays events that have happened more recently than the SMA line. Traders need the most recent information, not what has occurred in the past.

SMA Vs. EMA

At this point, let us consider which moving average is the most effective.

The EMA is a short period exponential moving average, which is best for when you need a rapid reaction to a price action.

EMA's strength lies in its ability to identify trends earlier, earning a large profit. This will be explained in greater detail later on, but it's enough to understand that early recognition of a trend means that you can ride it out for a longer period.

Unfortunately, the use of an EMA means the chance of getting faked out during a consolidation period.

Price spikes might appear to be trends because of how quickly the moving averages react to price. When this happens, the indicator occurs too quickly to be taken advantage of.

The opposite is true for the SMA. Simpler moving averages that are longer will give a smooth, slow price action response.

Over the long term this is better as traders can get a better concept of the overall trend.

It is possible to dodge fake outs, but this results in a slower response to price action. This hesitation could result in missing the entire trade or a beneficial entry price.

The fable of The Tortoise and The Hare is appropriate for this situation.

Imagine that the SMA is the tortoise because it is slow and so it is possible that it won't manage a speedy start on a trend. On the other hand, however, the fail safes that characterise the SMA (a hard shell) prevent fake outs occurring on your trades.

This means that the EMA is the hare, who is of course faster than the tortoise. Trends can be recognised earlier but there is a much greater risk of fake outs.

The pros and cons of SMA and EMA are detailed below:

Pros

Smoother charts can help eradicate fake outs.

They provide the most recent price swings and up to date information.

Cons

Due to slow movement a delay may occur.

There is the chance of problematic wrong signals and fake outs.

Each trader needs to decide which moving average is the best for their strategy.

To ensure an objective approach, traders will usually plot several moving averages. A short EMA is the best approach for identifying the optimum time to enter a trade, while a long SMA can give a better impression of the trend.

Moving averages are useful for determining trading strategies. They are good for testing several time periods and can analyse each one. With experience, a trader can learn which one best suits their trading style. To begin, it is beneficial to try to use moving averages to locate the trend.

This is done by simply plotting one moving average on a chart. The price action will usually be found on the top of the moving average in an uptrend. The opposite is true for a downtrend, where the price action is located under the moving average.

Finding a Trend Using a Moving Average

Method to find and confirm trends:

This is the one way to check your trading instinct. The basic method of using a moving average to determine the trend is the price crossover.

- When price cuts from below the moving average to above it, it implies a bullish trend.
- When price crosses from above the moving average to below it, it suggests a bearish trend.
- Sloping upwards – Bull trend
- Sloping downwards – Bear trend

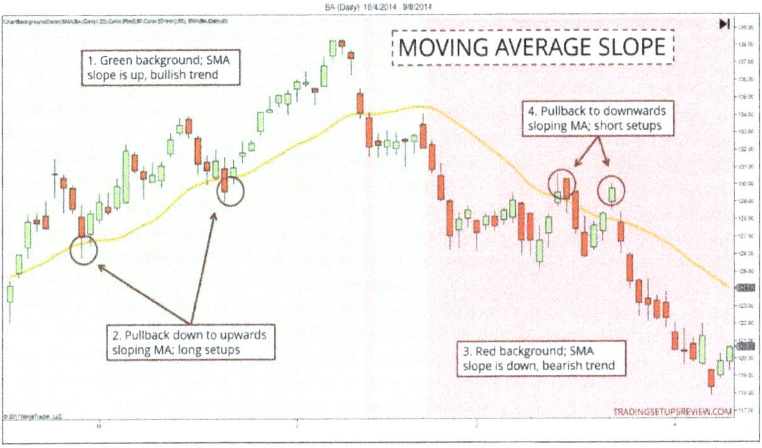

Most traders prefer to plot many moving averages as, due to the way that moving averages are ordered at any one time, this provides a better picture of downtrends and uptrends.

When moving averages are employed it should be possible to see uptrends and downtrends appearing in pairs. When the trend lines are recognised, the choice can be made whether to short or long a currency.

A minimum of three moving averages plotted are necessary to identify a downtrend or an uptrend pair, but the lines need to be in order still as a downtrend is slow to fast and an uptrend is fast to slow.

The procedure for inserting moving averages to a chart to identify a trend should now be clear. This information can highlight where the trend is and if it is likely to reverse or end. This is done by plotting a pair of moving averages onto the chart and waiting until a crossover appears.

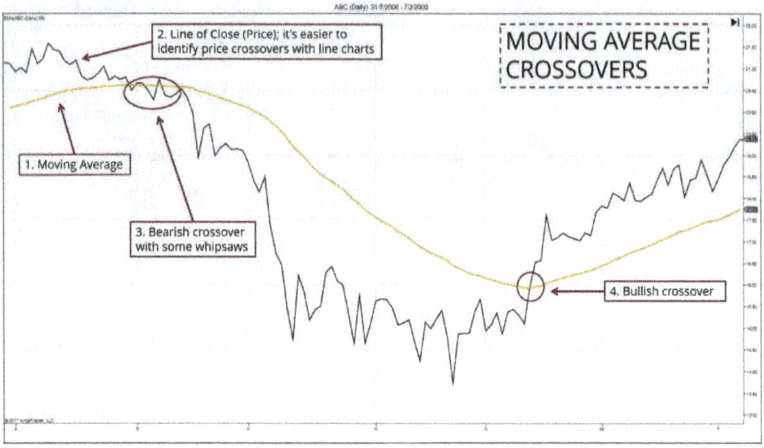

This is useful for spotting the best entry because a moving averages crossover is a sign that a trend may soon change. As we know, the better the entry, the better the chance to earn profits.

Rash judgements should not be made because the trade was not certain. Stop losses need to be taken into account along with consideration for where profit can be made. It is impossible to know how soon the next crossover will come along and spending too long waiting could cause greater harm.

This crossover system doesn't function as well, however, as it should in a trending or unstable market environment.

There is the opportunity, with a ranging price, of getting stopped out several times by coming across many crossover signals, prior to the chance of catching another trend.

There is the chance to use moving averages as dynamic levels of resistance and support.

They are known as dynamic because they operate differently from horizontal resistance and support lines. They fluctuate depending on the latest price action and traders usually use them as primary resistance or support levels. Traders tend to sell when they see the price rising to touch the moving average and then the price drops and tests a moving average, traders buy.

Using Moving Averages as Levels of Dynamic Resistance and Support

These always behave like normal resistance and support lines.

However, it is not certain that the price will achieve an accurate bounce off a moving average. Sometimes, the price temporarily goes over it, before continuing along in the trend direction.

The price can just go right past it, in other situations. It is possible to place two moving averages and buy or sell when the price occurs between them.

This space is known as a zone.

Forex traders make common use of this intraday or one-day tactics. Moving averages are areas, or zones, worth noting, similar to resistance and support horizontal areas.

This means that it is possible to consider the space between the moving averages as a resistance or support zone.

Broken Dynamic Resistance and Support

By now it should be possible to comprehend the methods of using moving averages for resistance or support. Using more than one creates a zone. They can also be broken, in the same way to all resistance and support levels.

At this stage you should understand how dynamic resistance and support levels occur from moving averages.

Below is a 1hr chart on the EURUSD showing the 20 EMA and how the price action related to it.

Touching the trend line in several locations offering entry points.

Below on the S&P 500 on the 4hr chart.

Offering multiple entry points both bull and bear positions.

Moving averages continuously change so it is possible to leave them running on the charts and not need to endlessly check the history to find potential levels of resistance or support.

This is because the moving interest area will always be denoted by this line. The issue now becomes making a decision to decide which is the most promising moving average to input.

A Summary of the Use of Moving Averages

There are several types of moving averages, but the most usual ones are exponential averages and simple moving averages. The latter is the easiest to use, but has difficulty with spikes.

The exponential moving average puts greater emphasis on the most recent prices and so recent trading activity is what is focused on here.

This has greater significance than prior events.

Simple moving averages, however, are smoother than exponential moving averages.

Short period moving averages are not as smooth as long period moving averages.

Although there is a greater risk of fake outs, an exponential moving average is much quicker at spotting trends.

Use of a smooth moving average can reduce the risk of fake outs and spikes, but this has a much slower reaction to price action. This delay in responding can leave you open to missing a good trade.

The end, enter point, and a trend can be found using a moving average. The moving average can help to locate the end, enter point and a trend.

A moving average is useful for making dynamic resistance and support levels.

If you plot more than just one type of moving average this results in the short-term and long-term movement being observed.

To see how moving averages operate it's a good idea to plot your own moving averages.

Using moving averages is not hard, but deciding on which moving average to use is. Using them yourself would be the best indicator of this.

It's up to you whether you use them as dynamic resistance or support levels, or you may rather use a system with trend-following.

The Use of Bollinger Bands

If you use a house as a metaphor for trading it is easier to explain what is commonly known as a trader's toolbox. When building a house, you need the right tools for each specific job, which is exactly the same for trading: traders need to use the most appropriate tools and indicators for specific situations and environments. If in doubt, more tools are best.

Your trading strategy determines if you will concentrate on one specific set of tools to trade in a certain environment. As with the building industry, trading specialists are necessary for each type of job. For example, you could be a specialist in moving averages, or an expert in Bollinger Band. It is possible to earn pips in infinite different ways.

Although you may not need all your tools for every job, at least you have them all in your toolbox. If you spot a favourable indicator you should try it out for yourself.

Bollinger Bands

A Bollinger band, named after its creator, John Bollinger, is a chart used to measure instability levels of the market.

The chart identifies how quiet or loud the market is – an expanding band means a loud market, while a contracting band means a quiet market. As the bands are close, on the chart below, this would mean a quiet price. When the price increases, the bands begin to spread.

There is a lot of background to these charts (calculations and formulas), but these are unnecessary when just beginning to use it.

What's much more important is how to use it for trading.

The website, www.bollingerbands.com, would be the best place to find all of the necessary information, including band calculation. The bands automatically widen when volatility increases and contract when volatility decreases.

The Bollinger Band Bounce

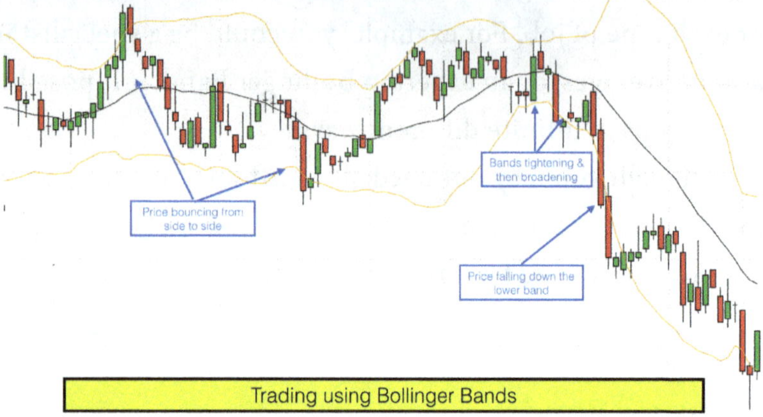

The price will usually travel to the middle of the two bands, when using the Bollinger band. It may seem wise to buy every time the price hits the lower band. Or, on the other hand, sell every time the price hits the upper band. This can technically work but is a risky way of trading using the Bollinger Bands. Sometimes strong trends will ride these bands and end up stopping out many unfortunate traders who used that method. This is why we are using the RSI indicator to help confirm and trade the "bounce" of an upper or a lower band.

You can make an entry when you see a STRONG BULLISH candle to the upside, consecutive reversal candles to the upside, or you find a bullish pattern forming. You need to see that the trend is moving upwards, in this case, before you enter a trade.

This would be a typical Bollinger bounce because the bands are behaving in a way that is the same as dynamic levels of resistance and support.

A longer timeframe will increase the strength of the bands. If there is no apparent trend and the markets are ranging, this strategy is commonly used by traders in their own methods that work well with bounces.

Bollinger Squeeze

Equation:

$$BBW = \frac{TBP - BBP}{SMAC}$$

where:

BBW = *BollingerBand*® width

TBP = Top *BollingerBand*® (the top 20 periods)

BBP = Bottom *BollingerBand*® (the bottom 20 periods)

SMAC = Simple moving average close
(the middle 20 periods)

Bollinger squeezes are a simple concept. The start of a breakout can be seen when the two bands begin to squeeze together, an upside bank break is bullish, while a downside band break is bearish.

A move usually continues going up when candles begin to appear above the top band. When the candles start appearing under the band at the bottom, this usually means that prices will continue to drop. Unconfirmed band breaks are subject to failure – again, use multiple tools!

Moves can be caught very early on with this method. They do not happen every day, but if you are using a 15-minute chart you might spot a few per week.

The two of the most common strategies of the Bollinger bands are the squeeze and the bounce, but these are not the only ones. Before progressing, make sure that the Bollinger band is put away in your toolbox.

Using a MACD Indicator

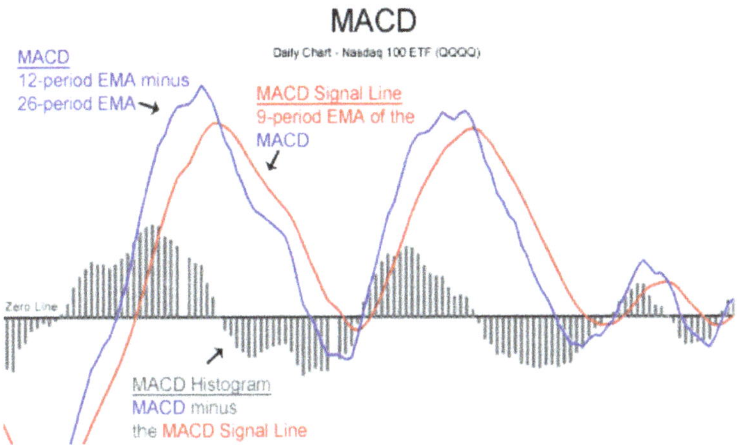

A moving average convergence divergence, or MACD, tool is a moving average that indicates a developing bearish or bullish trend. As we know by now, the main priority for earning profit is to identify trends.

You will come across three different numbers when setting your MACD charts.

For determining rapid moving numbers in the first number, you will use the first period number.

The second period number is used when you are determining the slow-moving averages.

The third number is obtained from the sum of the number of bars that you use to calculate the moving average difference of the slow and fast-moving averages.

If the MACD parameters were set to the default settings at 12, 26 and 9, it could be taken to mean the following:

12 is the first number and comes from the last 12 bars in the fast-moving average.

The second number, 26, comes from the last 26 bars in the slow-moving average.

The third number is 9 and this is taken from the last 9 bars.

This is plotted in the above chart by the two green vertical lines signifying the MACD, or histogram. A common misunderstanding about the MACD lines is that these green lines plot the price's moving average, but in fact they don't. The plotted moving averages are actually showing the difference between the two used moving averages and, in the example above, the fast-moving average above is the 26 and 12 point moving average difference. An average of the last MACD line can be observed by viewing the plot of the slow-moving average.

If we use the result of the previous 9-periods average from the fast MACD line, then we can get the slow-moving average. A line with greater accuracy can be obtained by doing it this way because the original line that we used was smoothed out.

The average of the slow and fast-moving averages has been plotted on the histogram. The histogram is seen to grow on the first chart as the moving averages diverge.

Due to this diverging of the fast-moving average from the slow-moving average, this is known as divergence.

Due to the moving averages moving towards each other, a smaller histogram is created. The fast-moving average converges towards the slow-moving average, so this is known as convergence.

This is how Moving Average Convergence Divergence came to be known as that. Now we know what MACD can do, it's time to see how you can use it.

How Trading Works with MACD

Each moving average has its own price movement reaction speed: the fast-moving average is fast; and the slow-moving average is slow.

When a new trend occurs, the fast line is the first to react and will move to cross the slow line. When this crossover happens, this is a sign of a possible new trend occurring, with the fast line diverging away from the slow line.

A downtrend has been accurately identified in the chart above because the fat line crossed beneath the slow line. When this happened, the histogram momentarily disappeared.

This happened because there was a zero difference between the two lines. Showing an increasingly strengthened trend, the histogram begins to increase in size as the fast line starts to diverge from the slow line, setting off the trend.

This example can be used:

When the EUR/USD rose, another uptrend began, and you could have earned 200 pips if you had gone long as soon as the crossover happened.

The MACD has one main flaw. As previously discussed, there is usually a lag between price and moving averages, due to it being based on previous price averages.

This occurs because it is a moving average, made up of moving averages, and then smoothed with a further moving average. It is still commonly used among Forex traders though.

Using the Parabolic SAR

our focus has primarily been on employing indicators that help identify the beginnings of rising trends in the forex market.

While recognising when a trend starts is vital for successful trading, it is equally important to understand when these trends are likely to conclude. A strong entry into a trade must be complemented by a clear exit strategy to maximise profits and minimise losses.

Understanding the Parabolic SAR

The Parabolic SAR, which stands for "Stop and Reverse," is an effective tool that aids traders in pinpointing potential trend reversal points in the market. The indicator is visually represented on your trading chart as a series of dots or points, which appear either above or below the price candles. These placements signify where you can anticipate changes in price direction.

When the Parabolic SAR points are located below the candles, it indicates bullish sentiment, suggesting that you should consider buying. Conversely, when the points appear above the candles, this signals a bearish trend, prompting you to consider selling. This straightforward interpretation makes the Parabolic SAR an accessible and efficient tool for both novice and experienced traders.

How to Trade Using the Parabolic SAR

Trading with the Parabolic SAR is notably simple and intuitive. As a retail trader, you can easily incorporate this indicator into your trading strategy. Here's how you can effectively utilise the Parabolic SAR in your trading decisions:

Identifying Buy Opportunities: When you notice that the Parabolic SAR points are below the price candles, this indicates a potential buying opportunity. For example, if the GBP/USD currency pair has its Parabolic SAR dots below the price action, it suggests that the market is in an uptrend. You might consider entering a buy order at this point, trusting that momentum will continue to push prices higher.

Identifying Sell Opportunities: Conversely, if the indicator shows the dots above the price candles, this suggests that it may be time to sell. For instance, if you are monitoring the USD/JPY pair and the Parabolic SAR has shifted, placing a sell order could be warranted, particularly if there's additional evidence of bearish momentum.

Establishing Exit Points: The Parabolic SAR not only helps you identify entry points but is also instrumental in setting exit strategies. If you entered a buy position when the dots were below the candles, you would want to monitor for any points that appear above the candles as a signal to close your position.

Practical Example

To illustrate this further, let's consider a practical example using the EUR/USD currency pair. If the price has been trending upwards, and the Parabolic SAR shows points consistently below the candlesticks, this indicates a strong bullish trend. As the price approaches a resistance level, you are vigilant for any change. If a new point appears above the candles, this could signal that the trend is reversing, prompting you to exit the trade to protect your profits.

Exiting Trades with the Parabolic SAR

The Parabolic SAR has another beneficial use: it helps identify if a trade should be kept open, or closed off.

Have a look at the daily EUR/USD chart above to see where the Parabolic SAR gave the sign to exit.

Towards the end of April, it appeared that the EUR/USD was going to keep dropping. Traders would have been concerned about how far down it would go, if they shorted now.

We can see that three points appeared at the start of June, which could indicate that that was a possible exit point for the shorts because it seemed to be the end of the downtrend. However, the pair rose back up around the 1.3500 point so those traders who had held, in the hope that the EUR/USD would continue to drop, would have incurred heavy losses.

Stochastic Indicator

This indicator is particularly effective for assessing whether a currency pair is entering oversold or overbought conditions, which can inform your trading decisions.

What is the Stochastic Oscillator?

The Stochastic Oscillator measures the momentum of price movements and uses a scale that ranges from 0 to 100. It consists of two lines: a fast line, often referred to as %K, and a slower line, known as %D. These two lines work in conjunction to provide insights into market conditions.

When the Stochastic Oscillator generates readings, it indicates how far the current closing price is from the price range over a specific period. A reading above 80 (represented by a red dotted line in charts) suggests that the market is overbought, signalling that prices may have risen too high and could be due for a correction or pullback. Conversely, when the oscillator falls below 20 (indicated by a blue dotted line), it signals oversold conditions, implying that the price may be poised for a rebound upward.

Using the Stochastic Oscillator in Forex Trading

The primary utility of the Stochastic Oscillator in forex trading lies in its ability to signal potential market reversals based on overbought and oversold conditions. For instance, if you observe the lines of the Stochastic Oscillator rising above the 80 level, this condition typically suggests that the currency pair you are trading may be overvalued. As a result, you might consider selling your position to take profits or to enter short trades in anticipation of a downward price movement.

Conversely, if the lines dip below the 20 level, this indicates oversold conditions. In this scenario, you could consider placing a buy order, expecting that the price is likely to rise as the market corrects itself.

Practical Application with an Example

To illustrate how you might use the Stochastic Oscillator in your trading, let's consider the analysis of the EUR/USD currency pair. You notice that the Stochastic Oscillator has been lingering above the 80 mark for an extended period. This suggests that the market has been experiencing excessive buying pressure. By observing the chart, you could make an educated guess that the price is likely to drop soon due to this prolonged overbought condition.

For example, if the price has reached 1.2000 and the indicator shows signs of declining from the overbought territory, you might decide to place a sell order, anticipating that the downward pressure will soon follow.

As you become more familiar with this tool, you may discover that it can help you identify divergences – when the price moves in one direction while the oscillator indicates another, hinting at potential trend reversals.

Understanding these nuances can greatly enhance your trading effectiveness and adaptability, offering you a broader range of strategies to employ based on your trading style.

RSI

The Relative Strength Index, commonly known as the RSI, is a popular momentum oscillator used in forex trading to evaluate the speed and change of price movements. This tool provides you with valuable insights into potential overbought or oversold conditions in the market, allowing you to make more informed trading decisions. While it has similarities to other indicators like the Stochastic Oscillator, the RSI offers unique benefits when analysing market trends.

How Moving Averages Work

Before diving into RSI, it's helpful to understand moving averages, as the concepts of smoothing out price movements and detecting trends connect closely with the use of the RSI. Moving averages are essential tools in technical analysis that help you smooth out price fluctuations over a specified time period. For example, you might calculate the average closing price of a currency pair, such as EUR/USD, over the past 10 days or 50 days.

When you display this data on a chart, you typically will see a price line representing the historical closing prices of the currency pair over time. Alongside this, you can plot additional lines that represent the moving averages – such as the 10-day and 50-day averages. These moving average lines help clarify trends, as they filter out market noise and highlight the overall direction of price movement.

Using the RSI in Trading

The RSI operates on a scale of 0 to 100 and is primarily used to identify potential tops and bottoms in the market, signalling whether a currency pair is either overbought or oversold. Generally, an RSI reading above 70 is interpreted as overbought, indicating that a reversal to the downside may occur. Conversely, a reading below 30 indicates that the market may be oversold, suggesting that a price increase could be on the horizon.

Determining Market Trends with RSI

In addition to identifying overbought and oversold conditions, the RSI can also be employed to confirm market trends, making it exceptionally popular among traders. To analyse trends using the RSI, observe the level of the index: if the RSI is below 50, this typically indicates a likely downtrend. In contrast, if the RSI rises above 50, it signifies a potential uptrend.

Consider a scenario in which you are analysing the GBP/JPY currency pair. If you notice that the RSI has remained below 50 for an extended period, this suggests that bearish momentum is prevailing in the market. You might decide to look for opportunities to enter short positions, capitalising on the anticipated continuation of the downtrend. Conversely, when the RSI crosses above 50, it may indicate that the tide is turning, prompting you to consider long positions as bullish sentiment begins to build.

To avoid false signals, it's advisable to wait until the RSI drops below 50 to confirm a downtrend or crosses above to affirm an uptrend.

Limitations of the RSI

While the RSI is a powerful tool, it is essential to acknowledge its limitations. The RSI can remain in overbought or oversold territory for extended periods, which may result in misleading signals. For instance, a currency pair might be classified as overbought and yet continue to rise for some time before a reversal actually occurs. This scenario can lead to premature trading decisions if you rely solely on the RSI without considering other market factors.

This can join the other tools in your toolbox. Experience will show you what tool to use for each situation to make the most informed decisions.

Bollinger Bands

This indicator is popular to measure market volatility and identify potential price levels where a currency pair may be overbought or oversold. Bollinger bands consist of three lines plotted on a price chart: the middle band, the upper band, and the lower band.

Middle Band: This is typically a simple moving average (SMA) calculated over a specified number of periods (commonly 20). It acts as a baseline for the bands and reflects the average price of the currency pair over the chosen timeframe.

Upper Band: This band is calculated by adding a set number of standard deviations (usually two) to the middle band. The upper band represents a level where prices may be considered overbought, suggesting that the market might need to correct downwards.

Lower Band: Conversely, the lower band is derived by subtracting the same number of standard deviations from the middle band. It indicates a level where prices may be seen as oversold, indicating a potential upward reversal in prices.

How to use Bollinger Bands

They are designed to provide insights into price volatility, trend direction, and potential trading opportunities. Below, we explore several ways you can utilise Bollinger Bands to inform your trading decisions.

Identifying Volatility

One of the primary uses of Bollinger Bands is to help you gauge market volatility. The bands consist of three lines: the middle band, which is usually a simple moving average, and the upper and lower bands, which are set a specified number of standard deviations away from the middle band.

When the distance between the upper and lower bands widens, it is a clear indication of high volatility in the market. This widening suggests that significant price action may occur, either to the upside or downside. Conversely, when the bands contract and come closer together, it signals lower volatility, often preparing the market for a potential breakout.

For example, if you are monitoring the AUD/USD currency pair and notice that the Bollinger Bands have widened significantly, this could suggest that the market is about to experience a substantial price movement. You may want to adjust your trading strategy accordingly, perhaps preparing to enter positions that exploit this anticipated volatility.

Spotting Trends

Bollinger Bands can also assist you in spotting prevailing market trends. Typically, prices move within the upper and lower bands. If the price frequently touches the upper band, it indicates that the market is in a strong upward trend, reflecting sustained buying pressure. In this scenario, you might consider taking long positions to capitalise on the ongoing climb.

Conversely, if you observe the price consistently touching the lower band, it suggests a downtrend, characterised by persistent selling pressure. In this case, you may want to look for selling opportunities or short positions as the market continues to decline.

Two notable strategies involving Bollinger Bands are the Bollinger Bounce and the Bollinger Squeeze. Both strategies harness the unique insights offered by Bollinger Bands, which consist of a middle band and two outer bands that encapsulate price volatility.

Bollinger Bounce Strategy

The Bollinger Bounce strategy relies on the concept that prices tend to return to the middle band of the Bollinger Bands after reaching either the upper or lower band. This middle band is usually a simple moving average (SMA) that reflects the average price over a specified period and serves as the core point around which price fluctuations occur.

In this strategy, if the price reaches the lower Bollinger Band, which typically indicates that the currency pair is oversold, you should consider placing a buy order. For instance, suppose you are monitoring the EUR/USD currency pair, and you notice that the price has touched the lower band at 1.1200. This could signal an opportunity to buy, anticipating that the price will bounce back towards the middle band, potentially reaching around 1.1250.

Conversely, should the price hit the upper Bollinger Band, which signifies that the asset may be overbought, it is advisable to consider selling. Continuing with the EUR/USD example, if the price reaches the upper band at 1.1300, you could enter a sell position, expecting the price to retrace towards the middle band.

It is important to note that the Bollinger Bounce strategy works best in a ranging market where prices oscillate between the upper and lower bands without establishing a clear trend. In such environments, the price tends to respect the bounds presented by the Bollinger Bands, making this strategy more reliable.

Bollinger Squeeze Strategy

In contrast, the Bollinger Squeeze strategy is highly effective for identifying potential breakouts in the market. A squeeze occurs when the Bollinger Bands contract, indicating a period of low volatility. This contraction suggests that the market is consolidating and is often followed by an explosive price movement.

During a squeeze, the narrow range signifies indecision among traders; however, it also implies that a significant breakout could be on the horizon. Once the price eventually breaks out, it will move sharply either above the upper band or below the lower band, signalling a potential new trend.

For example, if you are analysing the GBP/JPY currency pair and observe that the Bollinger Bands have contracted significantly, it indicates a period of low volatility. If the price then breaks above the upper band after this squeeze, it suggests that bullish momentum is taking over. You might then consider entering a long position to capitalise on the expected upward movement.

In conjunction with the Bollinger Bands, using additional indicators such as the Moving Average Convergence Divergence (MACD) can provide further confirmation of the breakout direction. The MACD is a valuable tool that helps you spot trends and any potential reversals.

Understanding MACD in Trading

To utilise MACD effectively in your trading strategy, you'll need to analyse the distance between a fast-moving average and a slow-moving average, as well as vertical histogram lines that represent the difference between these two. The MACD helps to track momentum shifts and can indicate when the fast line crosses above or below the slow line, signifying potential entry or exit points.

For instance, when the MACD line crosses above the signal line, it typically indicates that a new bullish trend is beginning, suggesting a good time for you to enter a long position.

Conversely, if the MACD line crosses below the signal line, it could be a sign to exit from your long position or enter a short position if the conditions suggest a bearish trend.

Parabolic SAR

Parabolic SAR, which stands for Stop and Reverse, is a widely used technical analysis tool that helps traders identify potential trend reversals in various financial markets, including forex and stock trading. This indicator is particularly valued for its straightforward nature and its ability to provide clear buy and sell signals.

The Parabolic SAR is represented on a price chart by a series of dots (or "points") that appear either above or below the price candles. The position of these dots offers insight into the current market trend and signals when it may be time to enter or exit a trade.

How Parabolic SAR Works

Trend Reversal Identification: As the name suggests, the primary function of Parabolic SAR is to indicate potential reversals in market trends. The indicator is designed to adapt and move with the price, trailing it closely.

Bullish Signals: When the points of the Parabolic SAR are positioned below the price candles, this signals a bullish (or upward) trend. In this scenario, traders may consider entering a long position (buying) as it indicates that the market is likely to continue rising.

Bearish Signals: Conversely, when the points appear above the price candles, it indicates a bearish (or downward) trend. This serves as a signal to sell or to close any existing long positions, as it suggests that the market may be poised for a decline.

The Parabolic SAR is most effective in trending markets – especially during long rallies or downturns – where it can provide reliable signals for entering and exiting trades. For instance, in a strong uptrend, the dots will progressively move higher as the price increases. Traders may use the indicator to trail their stop-loss orders just below the Parabolic SAR points, allowing them to lock in profits while also protecting against potential reversals.

Stochastic Oscillator

The Stochastic Oscillator operates on a scale from 0 to 100 and consists of two lines: the %K line and the %D line. The %K line represents the current closing price of an asset relative to its price range over a specified period, while the %D line is a moving average of the %K line. By examining these lines, traders can gauge whether an asset is overbought suggesting a potential price decrease or oversold indicating a potential price increase.

Interpreting the Indicator

Overbought Conditions: When the %K line exceeds the threshold of 80, it indicates that the market is overbought. This suggests that prices have risen significantly and may be due for a correction or decline. In such cases, traders might consider selling their positions or looking for shorting opportunities. For example, if the Stochastic Oscillator shows a reading of 85, it may imply that the asset has experienced excessive buying pressure, and a downturn could be imminent.

Oversold Conditions: Conversely, when the %K line falls below the level of 20, the market is considered oversold. This reading suggests that prices have declined excessively and may soon rebound. As such, traders may look for buying opportunities. For instance, if the oscillator registers at 15, it indicates that the asset is undervalued, prompting traders to consider entering a long position in anticipation of a price reversal.

The Stochastic Oscillator is most effective when used in trending markets or in conjunction with other technical indicators. For instance, a trader might combine the Stochastic Oscillator with moving averages to confirm signals. If the oscillator indicates an overbought condition simultaneously with a bearish crossover in moving averages, this may strengthen the rationale to sell or close long positions.

RSI

This highlights those oversold and overbought market conditions similar to Stochastic.

An RSI over 70 means the market is overbought so you should sell.

An RSI under 30 means that the market is oversold, so you should buy.

RSI is useful for verifying trend formations. If you are watching a trend form, hold until the RSI goes over (uptrend) or under (downtrend) 50 and then enter.

Using Chart Patterns

The next tool for your box is Chart Patterns.

Imagine chart patterns to be like land mine detectors: they can assist you when looking for chart explosions, even before they happen.

This is, of course, the source of huge profits.

Chart patterns are extremely useful as a warning system, which will make you want to use them all of the time.

In the following section we will go through the main formations and patterns that you will come across in charts. If the information is correctly interpreted, massive breakouts can ensue.

The plan would be to find a prospective large movement so as to earn profit while riding it out.

It is every trader's goal to earn money after all!

By detecting chart formations to find specific conditions we can predict when the market is about to breakout. Trading strategies will benefit from this because the chart formations can tell you if a price will reverse or continue on track.

Double Top

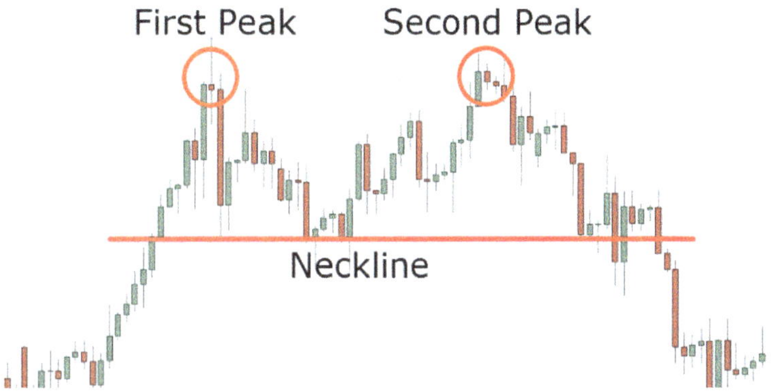

The double top pattern indicates a potential bearish reversal and serves as a key signal for you to adjust your positions accordingly.

Formation of the Double Top

A double top occurs when the price of a currency pair reaches a high point on the chart, subsequently pulls back to form a swing low, and then rallies again to approach the previous high. In simpler terms, after experiencing an extended upward movement, the price hits a particular resistance level that it struggles to exceed. This resistance level is referred to as the 'top' or 'peak.'

Importantly, the price tests this level twice: during the first attempt, it makes a new high, indicating strong buying pressure. However, the price then retraces, creating a swing low, before making a second, unsuccessful attempt to break through that same level. The classic definition of this pattern suggests that it is only deemed complete when the price falls below the swing low that was formed between the two peaks. At this point, it confirms that the buying pressure has diminished, signalling a potential reversal in the trend.

Visual Representation and Interpretation

When you examine a chart illustrating a double top, you will notice that the first peak is generally higher than the second peak, which serves as a crucial clue for your analysis. This phenomenon suggests that the momentum behind the buying activity is fading. As the price struggles to break through the resistance level during the second peak, it creates an opportunity for you to anticipate a reversal.

You should look for an entry point to sell just below the "neckline" of the double top pattern. The neckline is the support level drawn across the swing low that separates the two peaks. Once the price breaks below this neckline, it signals a more definitive shift in market sentiment, leading to further downward movement.

To illustrate this concept, refer to a chart where you can clearly see the two peaks following a prolonged uptrend. As the price declines after breaking through the neckline, you can confirm that your assessment of a potential bearish reversal was accurate.

Important Considerations

As you monitor the market for potential double tops, it's vital to remain vigilant for such formations, especially after a notable uptrend. Recognising these patterns early can allow you to position yourself effectively before the anticipated decline. By being attentive to the double top pattern, you can enhance your trading strategy and improve your chances of success in the forex market.

Double Bottom

Much like the double top pattern, the double bottom is an important technical analysis tool used to identify potential reversal trend formations in the forex market. Whereas the double top indicates a shift from an uptrend to a downtrend, the double bottom signifies a transition from a downtrend to an uptrend. In this case, instead of looking for opportunities to sell (go short), you would be looking to buy (go long) in anticipation of a price increase.

Formation of the Double Bottom

The double bottom pattern typically forms after a sustained downtrend. This pattern consists of two distinct "bottoms" that occur at approximately the same price level on the chart, creating a "W" shape. When the first bottom is established, the price briefly rises before declining again to create the second bottom. Importantly, the second bottom does not break below the first bottom; this critical characteristic suggests that selling pressure is diminishing. As a result, it implies that a reversal in the market may be imminent, allowing you to consider initiating a long position.

Visual Representation and Interpretation

When observing a double bottom on your trading chart, you will notice that both bottoms often occur at a similar price level, indicating strong support. This level represents a position where buyers are stepping in to prevent the price from falling further, effectively creating a solid foundation. Once the price action moves upwards and breaks through the neckline, which is the horizontal resistance level connecting the highs between the two bottoms, a positive move is confirmed.

For example, imagine you identify a double bottom formation at a price level of 1.1500. The first bottom forms when the price hits 1.1500, bounces up, and then drops again to 1.1500 for the second bottom. Once the price breaks above the neckline at 1.1600, this upward movement signifies that buying momentum is taking over, indicating that a bullish reversal is likely underway.

Height and Profit Targets

After the price breaks the neckline, it often experiences a sharp upward movement. Following this jump, it's worth noting that the price will generally reach a height comparable to the distance between the tops of the "W" and the neckline, providing a measure for setting profit targets. In our example, if the distance from the bottom to the neckline is 100 pips, it is plausible to expect the price to rise by a similar amount after the breakout. Hence, if you entered a long position at 1.1600, your target could logically be set around 1.1700.

Monitoring Reversal Patterns

Both double tops and double bottoms are essential tools in identifying reversal trends in the forex market. As a trader, you should be particularly vigilant for these patterns, especially at the end of a strong downtrend. Recognising these formations promptly can provide you with valuable opportunities to capitalise on potential price movements.

Head and Shoulders

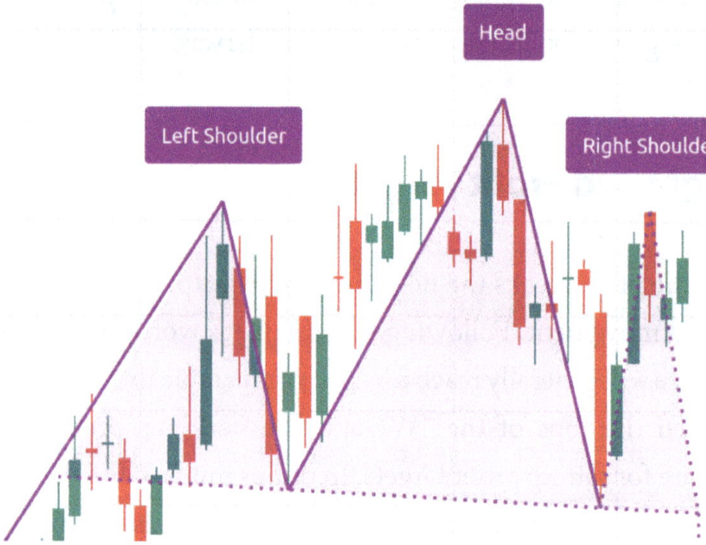

The head and shoulders pattern is a significant reversal trend formation that traders should closely monitor when analysing price movements in the forex market. This classic pattern signals a potential shift in market sentiment, indicating that a prevailing uptrend may be about to reverse into a downtrend. By recognising this formation, you can make more informed trading decisions.

Formation of the Head and Shoulders Pattern

The head and shoulders pattern is characterised by three distinct peaks: the first peak, known as the left shoulder; the second peak, which is the highest point of the formation and referred to as the head; and the third peak, called the right shoulder, which is typically lower than the head. To visualise this pattern, imagine a series of three hills, where the middle hill is the tallest, flanked by two shorter hills on either side.

To understand the full picture, you also need to observe the neckline, which is formed by connecting the two troughs that occur between the peaks. This neckline can slope either upwards or downwards, but a downward sloping neckline tends to provide a more reliable indication of a trend reversal.

For example, consider a forex chart where the price of a currency pair rises to create the first shoulder, then climbs higher to form the head before dipping back down and rising again to form the right shoulder. Once these features are clearly established, the head and shoulders pattern becomes apparent.

Recognising the Pattern in Action

In the graphic representation of the head and shoulders pattern, the head stands out as the highest point compared to the two shoulders. Importantly, the shoulders should not extend above the peak of the head. Once you have identified this pattern, it's crucial to determine where to place your trades effectively.

An entry order is optimally placed just below the neckline, which signifies the level where selling pressure may intensify, triggering a more significant price decline. For instance, if the neckline is at a price level of 1.2000, you might consider setting a sell order slightly below this level, anticipating that the price will drop following the completion of the pattern.

Calculating Targets and Managing Trades

To establish a profit target based on the head and shoulders pattern, measure the vertical distance from the highest point of the head down to the neckline. This calculated distance provides a guideline for how far you might expect the price to move once it breaks below the neckline. So, if the head is at 1.2200 and the neckline is at 1.2000, the distance is 200 pips. You can then project this distance downward from the point of the neckline break to set a potential target price.

When using the head and shoulders pattern in your trading strategy, it's essential to remember that price action can sometimes exceed the initial target. Nonetheless, it's wise to approach trading with caution rather than succumbing to greed. While it may be tempting to hold out for further gains, securing profits once you've reached your target can often be the best course of action.

Inverse Head and Shoulders

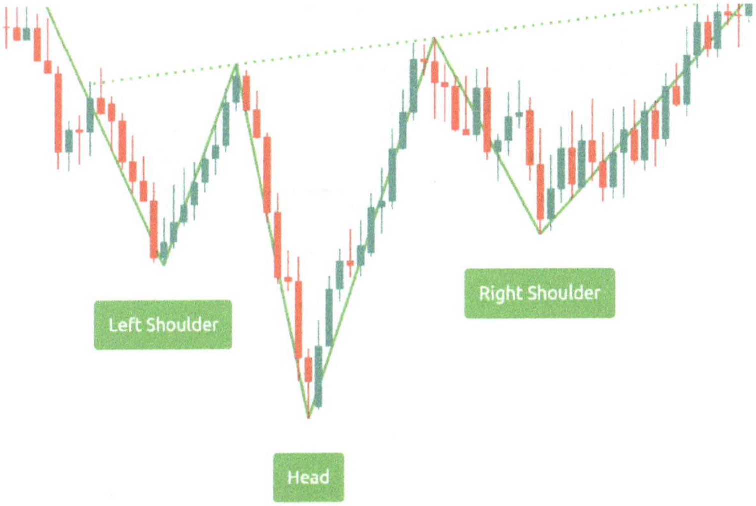

True to its name, the inverse head and shoulders is essentially the upside-down version of the standard head and shoulders pattern, and it plays a significant role in forex trading.

Formation of the Inverse Head and Shoulders

The inverse head and shoulders pattern typically emerges after a prolonged downward movement in price. This formation consists of three distinct valleys: the first valley represents the left shoulder, the second and deepest valley forms the head, and the third valley creates the right shoulder.

To visualise this pattern, imagine a shoreline where the first dip represents the left shoulder being formed. As the price continues to decline, it reaches a lower level to create the head before rising slightly and then falling again to form the right shoulder, which is higher than the head but lower than the left shoulder.

This pattern indicates that selling pressure is weakening and that buyers are beginning to gain control. Hence, recognising this formation can be pivotal for traders looking for opportunities to enter long positions in anticipation of a price increase.

Entry Signals and Execution

Once the inverse head and shoulders pattern has formed, it is essential to identify the neckline. The neckline is established by drawing a horizontal line at the peak of the two higher valleys (the shoulders). A long entry order should ideally be placed just above this neckline. For instance, if the neckline is at a price level of 1.3000, you would look to set your buy order slightly above this level, anticipating that the price will break through it confidently.

Calculating Your Profit Target

Setting an appropriate profit target after entering a trade based on the inverse head and shoulders pattern involves calculating the vertical distance from the neckline to the head. For example, if the head is located at a price of 1.2900 and the neckline is at 1.3000, the distance between these two points is 100 pips. Once the price breaks above the neckline, you can project this distance upward to establish your target price. Therefore, if you set your entry just above the neckline at 1.3005, your profit target could be set at 1.3105.

Observing Price Movement

When the price ultimately breaks through the neckline, you should observe a positive upward movement. For example, following the breakout, the price may begin to climb steadily, indicating that buyers are now in control of the market. As the upward trend continues, you stand to gain respectable profits if the price reaches your target.

Managing Your Trade for Continued Success

After entering the trade and watching the price move favourably, it is crucial to implement effective trade management techniques. As the price progresses in the desired direction, consider using trailing stop-loss orders to secure a portion of your profits while still allowing for potential further gains. This way, if the market experiences any volatility, you can protect the profits you've made while keeping the position open for additional rewards.

Using Wedge Patterns to Trade

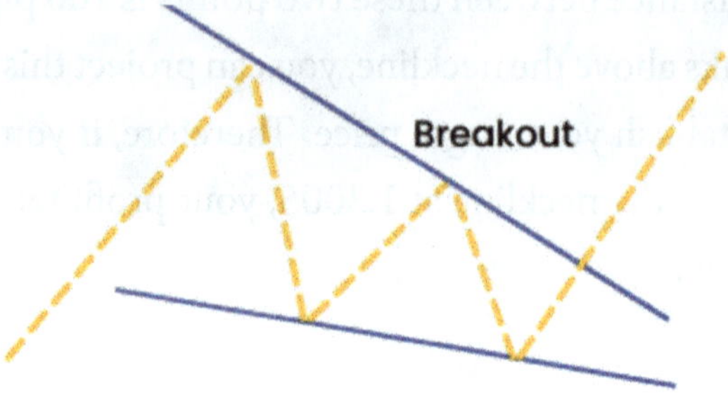

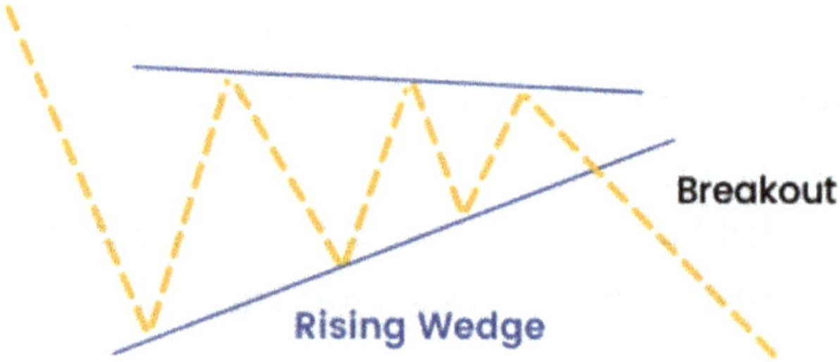

rising wedges alert traders to potential consolidations within an ongoing trend, indicating that there may be pauses or hesitation in the decision-making process among traders regarding the direction of the currency pair.

Understanding Wedge Patterns

Wedge patterns can signify both reversal and continuation scenarios in the market, making them important tools for any trader. The most relevant type for our discussion is the rising wedge.

Formation of a Rising Wedge

A rising wedge forms when the price action strengthens while the price moves between two upward-sloping lines – one representing resistance and the other representing support. The key distinguishing factor of a rising wedge is that the slope of the support line is steeper than that of the resistance line. This means that, although the price is making higher highs, it is doing so at a slower rate compared to the higher lows that are being created. The resulting shape creates a wedge, hence the name.

For instance, let's consider an observed price chart of a currency pair. As the price continues to ascend, it establishes a series of higher highs and higher lows. However, you would note that while each subsequent high is higher than the last, the price is beginning to rise more slowly. This price action creates the characteristic wedge shape.

Trading Signals from the Wedge Pattern

Identifying a rising wedge can be particularly valuable for predicting a potential breakout. When the price consolidates within the wedge formation, it often indicates that a significant price movement is imminent – either upward or downward. Specifically, following an established uptrend, a rising wedge formation typically leads to a bearish reversal pattern. This means that traders should prepare for a possible decline in price.

Alternatively, if a rising wedge forms during a downtrend, it may signal a continuation of that downtrend, indicating that the bearish momentum is likely to persevere.

Regardless of the market context, spotting a wedge formation should prompt you to take action and consider placing an entry order based on the anticipated breakout.

Example of Rising Wedge in Action

In our analysis of a hypothetical trading chart, we see the formation of a rising wedge at the end of an uptrend. The price manages to create new highs; however, the increase in price is gradual. Remarkably, when the price finally breaks below the support line of the wedge, it suggests that traders are favouring short positions instead of long ones. This shift typically indicates that the market sentiment is turning bearish, which can lead to a significant price drop.

As you monitor the chart, you may notice that post-breakout, the price tends to drop by an amount roughly equivalent to the height of the wedge itself. This attachment between the wedge height and the subsequent price movement is vital for setting profit targets and managing your trades effectively.

Distinctive Features of the Wedge Formation

A slightly different variant of the rising wedge can also occur, which signals a bearish continuation. In this scenario, following a downtrend, the price exhibits higher lows while simultaneously establishing lower highs. This pattern indicates that although the price is attempting to push higher, the prevailing downtrend remains dominant.

In this case, the chart reveals how the downturn continues after the price breaks downward, solidifying the continuation signal. When measuring the height of the wedge, you will find that it corresponds to the downward movement the price underwent after breaking through the support level.

Falling Wedge

As with a rising wedge, a falling wedge can either provide a continuation signal or a reversal signal.

To signal an upcoming trend, the reversal signal will appear on the bottom of a downtrend.

The continuation signal will appear during the downtrend to mark a continuing upward moving price action. The falling wedge is bullish, while the rising wedge is bearish.

With a falling trend line, the line that connects the highs is steeper than the line that connects the lows.

The pair have travelled upwards to the approximate same height as the formation, having broken through the top of the wedge. This chart shows how the result was the rally finishing up by a few pips past the target.

The wedge is performing as a continuation signal in the example shown below. To recap, falling wedges that form while the uptrend is ongoing usually behave as an indicator for a trend that could carry on later.

In this chart, the falling wedges are performing as reversal signals. As soon as the downtrend had finished, the price created lower lows and lower highs.

When the strong rally ended, there was a time when the price strengthened. It is possible that this occurred because the buyers paused following a large trading session, while recruiting more traders for the trade at the same time.

The charts show the pair preparing for a strong movement. The difficulty is identifying what direction it's going to take.

In this case the chart demonstrates a price climb, following its break of the top side.

Pips could have been earned on the strength of the uptrend, if a trader connected the highs of the pair by putting an entry order on top of the falling trend. The height of the wedge formation would have made a perfect upside target.

If you close off some of your position and permit the rest to ride, this will join some of your profits to the target, which could result in further pips earned.

A rectangle chart pattern will form when the price is bound by the parallel resistance and support levels.

This indicates that a phase of indecisiveness has happened among the traders as the sellers and buyers try and fail to take over the trade.

Prior to breaking out, the price will test the resistance and support levels several times. The price may then trend either upwards or downwards, contingent to the side the breakout was on.

When you catch a rectangle formation you need to think outside the box.

Trading Breakouts with Rectangle Chart Patterns

In the chart above we can see that with the key price levels the pair is bordered by the parallel lines. As soon as a level is broken, we can follow it.

Bearish Rectangle

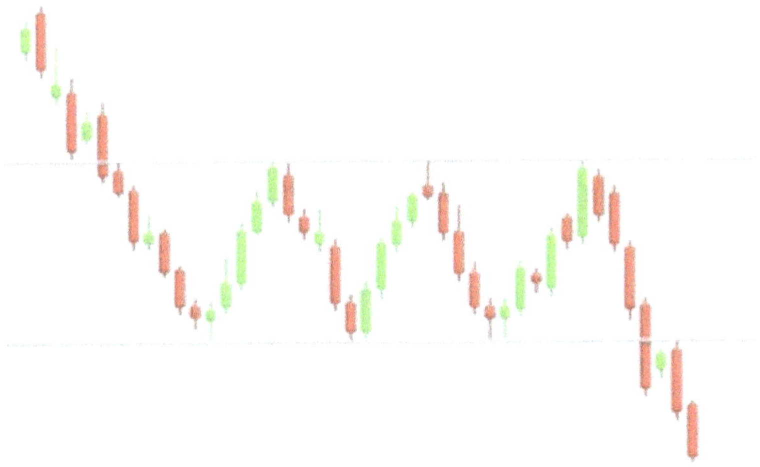

This formation often arises when there is a period of price consolidation, during which traders may pause to re-evaluate their positions before making a decisive move to push the currency pair lower.

Formation of the Bearish Rectangle

A bearish rectangle pattern is characterised by a horizontal price range that forms between two parallel support and resistance levels. During a downtrend, the price may briefly stabilise, leading to a series of minor highs and lows, creating the rectangle shape on the chart. This consolidation phase reflects a balance of power between buyers and sellers, but it is essential to recognise that the overall trend remains bearish.

As traders hesitate during this period, some may be considering further selling opportunities while others might be reluctant to commit. Once the price reaches the lower boundary, or support level, of the rectangle and breaks through, it typically signals a continuation of the downward trend.

Interpreting the Price Movement

When the price ultimately breaks below the support level of the rectangle pattern, it often leads to a rapid decline. This movement opens a lucrative opportunity for traders who placed short orders just below the support level prior to the breakout. For example, if you are analysing the GBP/JPY currency pair and observe a bearish rectangle pattern forming, you might set a short position slightly below the identified support level, anticipating that the price will drop swiftly once this barrier is breached.

In the example scenario, if the price breaks through the support level, plummeting from 150.00 to 148.50, you stand to gain considerable profits due to the well-timed entry below the critical level.

Profit Expectations Based on Rectangle Size

An important aspect to remember when dealing with the bearish rectangle pattern is that the height of the rectangle can provide insights into the potential movement of the currency pair once it breaks below the support level. The larger the rectangle, the more significant the anticipated price drop. This relationship enables you to set realistic profit targets based on the distance of movement you expect following the breakout.

For instance, if the rectangle's height measures 100 pips, you might expect that after the breakout, the price could potentially extend an additional 100 pips lower from the support level. In our earlier example of the GBP/JPY pair, if your target was set at 148.00, this objective would align with the expected price movement based on the rectangle's height.

Bullish Rectangle

Another kind of rectangle chart pattern is the bullish rectangle. The chart above displays an example of the price pausing to gather strength for the uptrend ending. Try to determine the direction the price is going to take.

The answer is of course upwards and you can observe the upside breakout.

When a pair breaks it makes a move at least equal to its last range size. This is like the movement in the bearish pattern previously covered.

From the chart we can observe how the price rose dramatically as soon as it broke through the top of the rectangular pattern. If the resistance level had maintained a longer order at the top, pips could have been gained on the trade.

Using Bull and Bearish Pennants to Trade

A pennant can form as soon as a strong move ends. This is a continuation chart pattern, similar to the rectangle patterns.

When a large downtrend or uptrend ends, a pause usually occurs and a pair will usually head off in the same direction once again. This price consolidation creates a small symmetrical triangle, known as a pennant formation.

A bearish pennant is formed when there is an almost vertical downtrend. The price tends to consolidate following this, due to several sellers closing and joining.

When the sellers re-enter the trade, this causes the price to carry on downwards once it has broken under the pennant's bottom.

The drop continued as soon as the price completed its breakout through the bottom. To trade on this pattern, it would be best to place a stop loss over the top of the pennant and a short order on the bottom. This would avert the chance of a fake breakdown and the risk of getting stuck in the trade.

A pennant forming is a sign that a stronger move is on the way. This movement will be different from the others in that its height will not be in comparison to its formation height. The height of the mast, or earlier move, will give a good indication of the rough size of the move the breakout might make.

Bullish Pennant

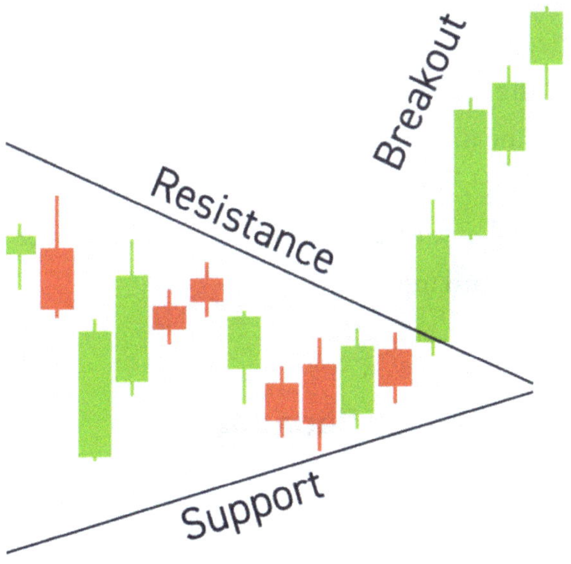

This pattern emerges during a period of consolidation, where price movement stabilises following a significant upward advance. The bullish pennant serves as a signal that a sharp price increase is likely approaching, reflecting the energy that the bulls are accumulating to push prices higher.

Formation of the Bullish Pennant

The bullish pennant pattern is characterised by a price movement that initially rises sharply, formed by a strong uptrend, before entering a consolidation phase. During this period, the price takes on a triangular shape, with converging trend lines that showcase a narrowing range of price movement. This consolidation represents a gathering of strength by the bulls as they prepare to make another charge upward.

For example, consider the GBP/USD currency pair. You might notice that after a substantial rally pushing the price up to 1.4000, the price then consolidates between 1.3900 and 1.3950, forming the pennant shape as buyers and sellers dispute control. Although the price has temporarily paused, it's essential to understand that the bulls are simply regrouping their strength for another upward move.

Trading the Bullish Pennant

As the bullish pennant formation approaches its apex, you should prepare for a potential breakout to the upside. Once that breakout occurs, you'll notice a decisive movement beyond the upper trendline of the pennant, validating the bullish sentiment in the market. To effectively trade this pattern, it is advisable to place a long order just above the top of the pennant. This allows you to enter the market as soon as the bullish momentum resumes.

Additionally, to manage risk, you should consider setting a stop-loss order just below the bottom of the pennant. This will help protect your position from potential false breakouts or market reversals, allowing you to limit your losses should the market move against you.

Notably, the height of the initial price movement preceding the pennant, often referred to as the "mast," can provide valuable insights when forecasting the size of the upcoming breakout. This height can guide your expectations regarding how far the price might rise following the breakout.

Using Triangle Chart Patterns to Trade

Similar to the bullish pennant, triangle patterns are essential tools in the forex trading toolkit, particularly symmetrical triangles. A symmetrical triangle is formed when the slope of the price highs and the slope of the price lows converge. This pattern occurs as the market creates higher lows and lower highs, indicating a conflict between buyers and sellers where neither group fully asserts control to generate a clear trend.

During this phase of consolidation, the price movement tightens, and the distances between the highs and lows narrow, creating the triangle shape on the chart. While this indicates that a breakout is forthcoming, it does not provide a clear indication of which direction the price will move.

Anticipating Breakouts

The key to successfully trading triangle patterns lies in your ability to place entry orders strategically. You should consider placing an order just above the resistance level formed by the declining highs, as well as another order just below the support level formed by the rising lows.

By doing this, you position yourself to take advantage of a breakout in either direction, whether the price moves upward or downward. If you observe that sellers are struggling to push the price down in your analysis of the AUD/USD pair, the result might be a series of higher lows and lower highs, indicating the static nature of the market. Should the price break above the upper resistance level of the triangle, having an entry order set there allows you to profit from upward momentum.

Ascending Triangle

The ascending triangle chart pattern is useful for locating higher lows slopes and levels of resistance.

The resulting pattern is due to the buyers not being able to take the price over a particular level. It does still increase, and we can observe the slow upwards incline by the occurrence of higher lows.

All we have to do now is determine the direction it's going to take, and if the buyers will be able to break the level or encounter a resistance strong enough to stop them.

The formation of the higher lows would indicate that the buyers are making headway and increasing in strength. The chance of a breakout is good because of the amount of pressure being placed on the levels of resistance.

It is usual to hear of buyers forcing the price through the resistance level.

This is not always the case because if the buying power is weak the breakout won't happen. Most of the time, the price will increase though. It's better to be ready for the unexpected.

If you use this model you should place the entry orders under the higher lows slopes and over the line of resistance.

If there had been a short order present under the bottom of the triangle, pips could be obtained.

Reversal chart patterns are vital tools in the forex trading landscape, as they provide crucial signals regarding potential changes in market direction. These patterns are particularly useful for identifying moments when an ongoing trend may be about to change course, allowing you to adjust your trading strategy accordingly.

Identifying Reversal Patterns

When a reversal pattern emerges during an uptrend, it may indicate that prices are poised to drop, suggesting a possible shift from bullish to bearish sentiment. Conversely, if a reversal pattern appears during a downtrend, this could signal an impending price increase, hinting that sellers may be losing their grip on the market.

To capitalise on these signals, it is essential for you to place your orders in the direction of the anticipated new trend. For example, the neckline of the chart pattern will serve as a guiding indicator when determining your trading entry. A wise target to aim for is typically positioned near the height of the formation you are observing.

Example of the Double Bottom Pattern

For instance, consider the double bottom pattern, which is a common reversal formation. To identify this pattern, you would look for two distinct troughs (or bottoms) that occur at approximately the same price level, separated by a peak in between. Once you spot this pattern, your target price should be set based on the height of the formation. Specifically, calculate the difference between the neckline (the price level that connects the peaks between the two bottoms) and the lowest point of the bottoms. This height serves as a guide for potential upward movement once a breakout occurs.

When placing your orders, it would be prudent to set a long entry order at the top of the neckline. Moreover, to effectively manage your risk, you should consider placing a stop-loss order in the middle of the formation. This precaution ensures that you protect your capital in the event the market moves against your position. To calculate the appropriate stop-loss size, measure the difference between the neckline and the double bottoms, then divide this figure by two.

Continuation Chart Patterns

In contrast to reversal patterns, continuation chart patterns signal a potential restart of the prevailing trend. These patterns are often referred to as consolidation patterns because they represent a period where buyers and sellers are taking a pause, preparing for the next price movement. Essentially, they suggest that after a period of indecision, the trend will continue in the same direction it was headed prior to the consolidation.

Various continuation patterns exist including rectangles, pennants, and wedges. These patterns can serve dual purposes – some wedge formations may act as continuation signals, while others could reflect possible reversals, depending on the context of the trend they are situated in.

To effectively trade using continuation patterns, you need to consider the existing market direction and place your orders either above or below the formation. For instance, if you are analysing a pennant formation, you might look to set your target based on the height of the "mast," which is the distance from the lowest point to the highest point before the consolidation pattern began.

When employing continuation patterns, it is typical to set your stop-loss orders just above or below the respective chart formation. If you are trading a bearish triangle pattern, it would be prudent to place your stop-loss a few pips above the resistance or the peak of the rectangle.

Bilateral Chart Patterns

Bilateral chart patterns present a slightly different trading scenario as they indicate the possibility of price movements in both directions, making them more challenging to interpret. An example of this is triangle formations, where the price can potentially break either to the upside or the downside.

When trading bilateral patterns, it is beneficial for you to set entry orders at both the top and bottom of the triangle formation. This setup allows you to take advantage of whichever direction the price ultimately breaks out towards. You could feel a sense of excitement knowing that whichever way the price moves, you are prepared to act.

TRADING MISTAKES

There are certain mistakes that, regardless of experience, traders will commonly make. In order to avoid these pitfalls, we must first be able to identify them.

Fear of Missing Out

The fear of missing out, commonly known as FOMO, is a psychological phenomenon that affects many traders in the forex market. This feeling can compel you to enter a trade impulsively, driven by anxiety that you might miss a potentially lucrative opportunity. While it is natural to desire profit and to want to act quickly when you see a promising trade setup, succumbing to FOMO can lead to hasty decisions that may have serious consequences.

The Dangers of FOMO in Trading

When you allow fear of missing out to dictate your trading behaviour, it often results in entering positions without conducting adequate analysis or consideration of the existing market conditions. For instance, you may observe a currency pair experiencing a sharp price increase, leading you to enter the market in haste. If the timing is unfavourable, you could find yourself buying at the peak of a spike. This is particularly risky because prices may not sustain these highs, and once the more disciplined traders begin to sell, the price can dramatically drop.

Imagine you are tracking the USD/CAD pair, which has been experiencing a significant price rally. In a moment of FOMO, you decide to invest without fully analysing the trend. The price spikes to 1.3000, and you hurriedly place your buy order. Shortly after your entry, the price starts to retreat as market sentiment shifts, and you see the value of your investment drop because you entered too late. This scenario highlights how acting on impulse can lead to unnecessary losses, causing frustration and potentially undermining your confidence in your trading abilities.

The Importance of Following a Trading Strategy

To combat the negative effects of FOMO, it is crucial to adhere strictly to your trading strategy. A well-defined trading plan should include entry and exit points, risk management measures, and rules for analysing potential trades. By following your strategy, you position yourself to make more rational and informed decisions rather than allowing emotions to drive your actions.

It's also essential to be patient with your chosen entry point. If a price is hovering around your planned entry level, it may be tempting to rush in at a higher price if you're concerned about missing out. However, following your original plan is vital. Entering at an inflated price based on fear can lead you to deviate from your strategy and ultimately increase your risk of loss.

Example of Managing FOMO

For instance, suppose you have identified a buy signal for the AUD/JPY pair at 78.50 based on your technical analysis. As the market fluctuates, the price hovers around your entry point before moving slightly upward to 78.75. If you feel anxious about potentially missing out on a bullish move and decide to enter the trade at 78.75, you may inadvertently place yourself in a less advantageous position. Instead, if you had been patient and waited for the price to drop back to or below 78.50, you would be positioned for a more favourable entry that aligns with your trading strateg

Not Moving Your Stop Loss

Failing to adjust or relocate your stop loss can expose you to significant financial losses, undermining your trading efforts and potentially leading to a detrimental impact on your overall capital.

The Risks of Not Moving Your Stop Loss

When you enter a trade under favourable market conditions, it is essential to protect that trade through effective stop-loss management. If your trade begins to yield profits – let's say the market moves in your favour, showing an increase of at least 40 pips – you should consider moving your stop loss to break even. This adjustment can safeguard your investment and ensure that you do not incur a loss if the market unexpectedly reverses.

For example, if you entered a position on the EUR/USD currency pair at 1.1000 and the price rises to 1.1040, the natural inclination is to revel in the profit. However, if you fail to adjust your stop loss to at least 1.1000 (your entry point), you risk losing all your gains if the market reverses sharply. Instead, by moving your stop loss to break even once you've secured a 40-pip profit, you protect your capital and eliminate the possibility of losing on that trade.

Implementing a Locking Strategy for Profits

A practical strategy to further secure your profits involves "locking" them in as the market advances. For instance, you could adjust your stop loss upwards by 10 pips for every 20-pip increase in the market. Continuing with the EUR/USD example, if the price rises to 1.1060, you would move your stop loss to 1.1030. By employing this approach, you can gradually secure your profits while still allowing room for further upward movement.

The Importance of Strategic Consistency

One of the most critical lessons in trading is that inconsistency can be detrimental to your success. Changing your trading position or strategy based on short-term market fluctuations can lead to rash decisions. The worst outcome, however, is trading without a clear and structured strategy at all.

A well-defined trading strategy is built upon thorough analysis and informed by your market experience, allowing you to identify potential errors and adjust your position accordingly.

Averaging Down

Averaging down is an accidental error made by traders that has become more of a habit than a concentrated effort. There are several aspects to this, the main one being where the trader holds on to a losing position. This results in a loss of money, but in hand a loss of time, both of which could be better spent on a stronger trade position.

Due to your losses, you then need to earn a greater return on the rest of your capital to recover your losses. For example, if you lose half of your capital you will need to make a 100% return to recover your full capital amount. This shows how much you need to make to recover from heavy losses and you could find that, in the case of large amounts lost, it could take you quite some time to recover.

Averaging down works in the short-term, but eventually the outcome is a margin call or large loss because a trend will continue for far longer than a trader can remain liquid. This is particularly true for traders who add in additional capital as their position moves even further out of the money.

Day traders are even more exposed to this due to their short trading window. This gives them only a short time to seize opportunities as soon as they happen and to get out of any bad trades quickly.

Taking A Pre-Position For News

As we have seen previously, important news events can cause a stir in the financial market, although it's not so certain what direction this movement will take. Even experienced traders may assume that they know the direction the markets will take but they cannot guarantee it.

Sometimes, statements of intent or additional figures released in these bulletins can have the effect of sending the markets off in an entirely unexpected direction.

Sometimes the market shows signs of great instability, which can lead to all sorts of orders being placed and stops being set off on both sides. This results in a whipsaw action which is apparent prior to any clear trend materialising. Just remember that a trend may not occur in the short-term.

This is why you should not take your position prior to the release of any news broadcasts because you may be jumping the gun and putting your trading position at risk. Traders who expect to make easy money won't, and leave themselves open to heavy losses.

Trading Immediately After A News Release

When such announcements occur, traders often engage in assertive trading, reacting swiftly to the information at hand. While it might appear tempting to jump into the fray and attempt to make quick profits from market movements, it is crucial that you do not act without a solid and comprehensive trading strategy to support your decisions.

The Risks of Impulsive Trading

Diving headfirst into trades during volatile market conditions, particularly in response to major news announcements, can mirror the risks associated with holding positions prior to the release of those bulletins. Without adequate preparation and a well-thought-out plan, you expose yourself to substantial risks. Price movements during these periods can be unpredictable, and what initially seems like an opportunity for easy money can rapidly turn into a loss if the market does not move in your favour.

For example, imagine a scenario where a central bank announces a change in interest rates. In the seconds or minutes following the announcement, the market can experience extreme volatility. Traders may react impulsively, chasing movements without taking the time to assess the underlying fundamentals. As a retail trader, this kind of impulsivity can lead to significant financial setbacks if you don't have a strategy to mitigate the risks associated with sudden price swings.

Understanding Whipsaw Action

The period surrounding the release of important news often gives rise to what is known as whipsaw action in the market. This phenomenon occurs when there isn't sufficient liquidity in the market to absorb the volume of trades, leading to rapid price fluctuations known as hairpin turns. These abrupt changes can create challenges for traders, as prices can quickly spike in one direction only to reverse sharply shortly thereafter.

Even trades that initially appear profitable can suddenly flip back into the negative, resulting in unexpected losses. This occurs because the effectiveness of stop-loss orders heavily depends on market liquidity. In times of heightened volatility, like during major news releases, there may not be enough liquidity to execute your stop-loss orders at the desired levels. Consequently, this could lead to losses that exceed your initial expectations.

The Importance of Waiting for Market Stabilisation

In the aftermath of significant news releases, it is prudent for you to exercise patience and wait for the market to stabilise. This involves monitoring price activity and observing how the market reacts to the news. Once prices establish a more steady trend and the volatility begins to subside, you will be in a better position to assess the direction of the market confidently.

By adopting this approach, you reduce your liquidity risk and enhance your ability to manage other associated risks. After the initial shock of the news has dissipated, prices are more likely to follow a clearer trend, providing you an opportunity to enter trades with a higher degree of confidence.

Risking Over 1% Of Your Capital

Excessive risks do not guarantee an excessive return. Almost every trader who engages in high-risk trading will lose big at some stage. A wise rule to adhere to is to never risk more than one percent of your capital on a single trade. The majority of professional traders don't even risk that much.

You need to keep this in mind when day trading. You should establish a daily maximum amount that you are ready to risk. This amount shouldn't be more than 1% of your capital, or an amount equal to your daily average profit across a period of 30 days.

To show what we mean, have a look at the following: you have an amount of $50,000 so you can afford to lose a maximum of $500 per day. Or you can calculate this to equal your average daily gains.

For example, you earn $100 so you can keep the days when you lose $100 or under.

This will protect you from any one day or trade that can seriously damage your trading account. If you maintain a predetermined maximum risk amount of an amount equal to your daily average gain throughout a 30-day period, you can be sure that you won't lose a larger amount in one day or one trade than you can recover in another day.

Having Unrealistic Expectations

Unrealistic expectations can arise from multiple sources, but all the problems described above can occur as a result. Traders often expect certain things from the financial market that often don't materialise, and instead they need to accept that the market is inconsistent. It can be irrational and unstable and can trend in long-term, medium and short cycles. There is no way to separate every move and make a profit from every one. This is an unrealistic expectation and will lead to disappointment and mistakes.

Instead of impractical expectations, you should have a sound trading plan, and stick to it. If it works, don't deviate from your plan. With the influence on Forex trades, even the small profits can increase in size. Trust this, and as your capital grows over time you can increase the size of your position for greater returns. If you want to try out a new position, test it in small amounts first and if this looks promising, you can invest more into your strategy.

If you are intra-day trading all you can do is work with what you get during the day. It's worth noting that the markets are unpredictable when they open.

To combat this, you can make use of strategies that are effective early on, and might not work so well later in the day. As the day goes on it might go quiet and then you can put a different strategy into play. There may be a pick up in the market towards the end of the day, so you can try yet another strategy. If you can do this and embrace the volatility instead of obsessing over behaviour that cannot be guaranteed, you will trade better.

You may lose five trades in a row and incur losses. Traders at every level make a loss at some stage. However, if you alter your strategy when this happens all this does is drop you back to the start of your learning curve. Stick to your plan because all losing streaks have to come to an end eventually.

Don't forget to have a contingency plan for unexpected events. These can include a market collapsing, an important news bulletin or your internet is down, all of which can result in huge losses. Preparation is key and make sure a stop loss is in place. Traders who have their entire account wiped out have not prepared properly.

Even if current affairs are not your area of expertise, you still need to have some awareness of what's going on in the world.

If you just log on to your PC and jump right into trading, you are making an amateur's mistake as you have carried out no preparation nor established your trading plan for the forthcoming session.

Subsequent to any trade, analysis should be carried out to see how you got on. You can not only see where you were successful, but you can review any errors and learn from them going forward. This can help you when formulating your plan for the next day.

A successful trader maintains a journal of trades. Don't neglect this point!

If you chop and change between methods when your luck fails, this will lead to losses. There isn't any one perfect method – it's up to you to determine your own successes as your ability will make your own strategy successful.

Even if you identify a method that is consistently successful for you, you can't just sit back and wait for the money to roll in. The markets are in constant flux and as a trader, you need to keep up or risk heavy losses.

Don't regret your decisions. Professionals observe their data and use it to educate themselves going forward. They learn from their mistakes and remember them for their future strategies.

Long-term and short-term trading outlooks are very different, and not recognising and understanding this can cause you difficulties. With short-term trading anything is possible; you have zero control over your outcomes and no chance of forecasting the market. Long-term trading is completely different and formulating and adhering to a long-term goal can only make money.

What Do Traders Say?

Novice traders have several misunderstandings, which they believe to be true. The following section will examine these.

Some new traders believe that small stop losses equate to less risk because the distance of your stop loss influences the potential risk to your trade.

Risk is determined in relation to the prospective losses to your account. Your stopping distance is set in relation to your take-profit distance along with the size of your trade so as to get a clear picture of prospective risks.

Another misconception is that performance is measured in pips. This is not true as pips are completely random and are not a measure of performance. They are always subjective.

Dismissing the importance of the win rate and the risk: reward ratio when in actual fact these two together provide a trader with all of the information needed to determine the direction and performance of their future trades.

If someone claims to be able to guarantee you a set amount every day, it's a scam!

This omits the risks and chances of losses and does not give the full picture. Returns are never guaranteed and only quoted in percentages so to claim absolute figures is reckless and worthless.

Don't put the blame on algorithm trading and HFT if you are not making any profits. They are not the culprits. They are just innovative technologies that have altered how trading is carried out.

Don't blindly trust in price forecasts – there are no guarantees in trading! Some traders may occasionally get it right, but this is just luck – not foresight.

Be respectful. Using slang words such as boring, casino, killing it or firework indicate that you are only trading for the thrill of it. Markets are in constant flux: up and down; fast and low. You need to maintain a professional attitude and use the proper language that shows respect and removes emotion.

Using black and white terms such as 'always' and 'never' is not wise. Just because a trade has been profitable the last twenty times there is always the chance that the next time it will fail. Although the prices are still moving in your direction, this is no excuse for not using a stop loss or for maintaining a wider position.

Again, words such as "wish", "feel" or "hope" are inappropriate because you are letting emotions get involved. You cannot 'hope' that the market will perform in a particular way.

Analysis of the data is the only way that you are going to have any idea of what may happen.

Emotion has no place in trading and can result in heavy losses.

Risk And Money Management

Always watch a floating P&L when carrying out a trade. Watching the account move will cause you to trade emotionally.

If you spend too much time planning what to do with your profits or lamenting what could have been done with the money you lost, this should make you cautious about risking more than you can afford to lose. Trading large amounts will make you nervous and greedy, both negative emotions for trading. On the other hand, if you trade with small amounts, you may become careless about managing your risk and adhering to the trading rules.

Associations, links and relationships play an important role in your risk levels. Not paying attention to these can adversely affect your trades. In particular, you might think that trading tools often work better together, rather than individually, but in actual fact because they are so similar you might just be getting the same wrong answer in several different ways!

If you have a fixed stop-loss with an identical pip amount across several instruments, then you don't really understand trading. There are no shortcuts when going for success as success only comes with a solid stop loss tactic along with an awareness of the optimum time to enter into a trade.

Don't misjudge the importance of drawdowns or how likely they are. Traders who lose several times in a row blame the strategy. This is not the case.

Never add to a losing position. You need to accept that losses are part of the process and to deny this will destroy your account.

Set ups vary in quality so this needs to be taken into account when considering the size of your position. Don't take a risk on a 2% arbitrary number on every trade. Identify the different qualities of various entries and set ups and keep it professional when position sizing.

Spread is vital and only approximately 1% of day traders can guarantee a profit net of their fees. Spread is part of a trade's costs, so these need to be minimised.

The 'disposition effect' is where a trader usually sells a winning trade two times faster than they hold a losing trade (holding a loser and selling a winner).

The size of your account needs to be taken into account when trading as if it is too little or too large it can emotionally influence your trading decisions.

There is no getting away from the fact that maths and statistics are a necessary component of trading. They may be difficult and boring, but they need to be understood because trading is based on calculating the odds and managing probabilities.

Management Of Trades

A trading checklist is a vital tool for trading – especially if you are a novice. Going down through this list prior to commencing trade can noticeably improve your performance. Checklists are useful for steering you away from trades that don't match your criteria. This is good practice for discipline.

As much as you can, do not widen a stop loss order if you see that the price is starting to go against you. A stop loss is the point where you realise that your ideas aren't working out. Widening a stop loss order shows emotions and you are not just relying on your better judgement.

Do not use mental stop losses for increased flexibility. There is no benefit to be gained from them.

You should only ever pull a stop loss order to break even if it is a carefully thought out part of your trading strategy with analysis carried out to confirm that it is the correct course to take. Moving your stop loss to a break-even position would indicate that you are afraid of losses.

Don't move stops too close together because prices move in a wavelike motion so require breathing space. If you move them too close to a position at the most recent price, you are likely to exit trades that could otherwise have gone to a take-profit order. It is necessary to be able to tell the difference between a reversal and a minor retracement.

It is not recommended to use famous moving averages or round numbers to place a stop loss because prices react differently near round numbers and there is a higher occurrence of reversal frequencies in these places too. Professional traders know that retail traders can occasionally be lazy and pick the easy target. This means that they can use this to their advantage.

Common Sense

As we have already discussed, some traders believe that their inability to make huge profits is down to their choice of strategy. They hold the belief that if they can identify the right strategy, gain enough leverage and are lucky, they will strike it rich. This is not the case. Other traders who have lost consistently for endless months will blame it on their choice of strategy.

Trading needs to be treated as a professional pursuit. Although the basics are not difficult, there is still a certain amount of preparation work that needs to be put into it to return profits. Testing strategies, gathering and analysing data, making continuous tweaks and self-improvements, organising, journalling and, above all, having discipline and hard work, without which, a trader cannot make money.

Some traders can't be bothered to maintain the background preparation necessary for successful trading, so they pay for a $10 Expert Advisor. This is a trading robot that claims to do all the hard work for you. The traders put too much reliance on it without understanding the background, and begin trading.

Despite a price remaining in a rally for several months, there will always be traders who believe that a turn is imminent and look for short-term trades. Traders should concentrate on what is in front of them and join a trade for as long as possible.

Be wary of traders who use their own savings and money following just three months of use of a demo account.

Obviously, there are many opportunities in trading; however, there are huge risks, and if you use your own money to trade following only three months of varied results, you can expect an impending margin-call.

To reiterate a previous point: it's not the choice of strategy that you use that increases your chance of success, it's the way that you use it. It doesn't matter the type of strategy that you use, following indicator-based strategies or trading on price actions, it's how the boundaries are negotiated and your own performance while trading that matters.

It's not wise to take a full account of your situation at the end of each day. Profit is not guaranteed every day, week or month because trading is a long-term activity and you cannot determine your trading outcomes. Your job is to determine the strategy that works best for you, stick with it and constantly analyse your performance. Winning trades cannot be forced as the market will always do its own thing.

Don't base your position on advice from a stranger, regardless of how certain the tip, guarantee, tweet or judgement is.

OVERCOMING DIFFICULTY

Putting too much effort into being correct

Everyone wants to be right but obsessing over this can actually be a negative action; you will seem needy. In extreme circumstances the need to be right can dwarf common sense and you can overlook what's right in front of you. This obsession to be right can indicate a lack of confidence, which your brain will pick up on and cause negative thoughts.

Negativity can be cured by actual confidence in your hard-won abilities and can help you make sound, rapid trading decisions. Improving your confidence can overrule the majority of trading errors.

Negative concerns that you are experiencing about your performance will subconsciously make their way to the surface. This can materialise in negative influences on your abilities. Working on your confidence can boost your emotions, which will positively improve your performance and thoughts, increasing your ability to trade efficiently.

Acting in a way that doesn't reflect who you are

It is a mistake to create an image in your mind of a 'perfect' trader and to then try and emulate this. It is not wise to try and make yourself into something that you are not and actually doesn't even exist. Regardless of how great it might seem to reinvent yourself as this ideal, it's a disaster to try to be someone you are not.

If you base your judgement on this false persona, you will lose faith in yourself. The level of pressure it takes to maintain this façade at all times is immense and can leave you feeling unsteady and doubtful of your own abilities. If you can't trust yourself then you lose confidence, which makes it almost impossible to use sound judgement to make informed decisions and instead take a riskier course of action.

Be yourself. You can make use of your own skills and abilities and give them free reign to develop. Reliance on yourself will give you the confidence to make your own way in the financial markets and to make use of your own way of doing things.

Think about it.

An awareness of your own capabilities, strengths or weaknesses, can be useful for recognising what makes you unique. You can appreciate where you are strong and trade well, and you can understand where you need to work harder. A contemporary trader's greatest tool is the ability to trust oneself and to remain true to your personality, no matter what.

Making choices based on a situation you don't fully understand

Making uninformed, snap decisions with no background research is never a good idea. It's a common mistake, regularly made.

This is not a guessing game. The professional trader will never assume. Instead they will assess the information available to them and make their decisions based on that.

Don't base your trading plan on the short-term picture in front of you. Trading is a long-term pursuit and putting your faith on pre-judgement could lead to losses because you moved too early.

Always wait and consider the situation. Watch as the situation unfolds and gather any additional information along the way before making a decision. Don't jump into reckless decisions, take a look at the bigger picture, which may be very different from what you originally thought.

Too much action, not enough evaluation.

Nerves can lead to hasty trading by trying to hide them through reckless bravery. This may work in the short-term, but, next thing you know, you are forgetting to carry out your preparation work and you are no longer making decisions based on information and judgement, but on what must be done next.

Use your tools. Give them the chance to work before writing them off as ineffectual. If you do you can relax and absorb the market data that you have collated and formulate your trading strategies on any new data gained.

Proper use and faith in the tools helps you to make the right decisions. It relieves some of the stress and shares the decision-making burden.

Not keeping control of trades

It's perfectly reasonable to take your time when considering a set up initially. Careful consideration takes time.

However, don't take too long because you will lose the edge of trusting your decisions and becoming reactive. Keep control and continue to analyse.

Maintain control. Prepare any questions you feel are relevant to the upcoming trading period so that you can be prepared to make your decisions without delay. This level of control will keep your progress moving and will help maintain a level of calm.

Getting Rid of Clutter from Its Origin

Coming from a large family can be a wonderful experience but one of the main problems associated with this is the huge volumes of clutter that can accumulate over time. Many siblings collecting stuff combined with parents who like to save stuff while constantly purchasing can lead to problems. Adults from this type of background often find it cathartic to make the transition to a clutter-free existence later on in life.

They may find, however, that much of the clutter retained is not physical, it is mental. This is much harder to let go of.

It may only take a life-altering event to recognise what the negativity is doing to you and the loss of your stability and lucidity may be lost because of it.

Clutter begins in your mind so if you decide to declutter your life, this is where you must begin. However, the question here is 'how can you declutter what you cannot see?'.

To begin a mental declutter begins with acting more intentionally, concentrating on the most efficient use of your time and energy, and directing your attention towards the areas where it is most needed.

There are 10 easy to implement tips that you can utilize to start on the path to a less cluttered mind.

1. Remember to log why you are thankful

Thankfulness is a display of how grateful you are for all that you have received or have earned. Thankfulness and gratitude show that you are satisfied with your lot in life and that you don't need more to be happy. To obtain balance in your life take the time each day to consider the blessings that you have.

When you take the time to feel grateful you are less likely to feel angry.

You should take a regular five minutes to journal five different reasons for feeling grateful. These reasons can be big or small and can vary from winning a prize, being grateful for your seatbelt, or getting to spend time with your family. The choice is yours.

2. Keep a journal of your thoughts

A good practice to help to deal with thoughts is to write them down. This can be done on a paper journal or an electronic one.

Just the physical act of listing out your dilemmas can sometimes help you to put them in order and give you a positive output for your concerns, dreams, experiences and passions.

Sometimes, writing down your thoughts can help you to take a step back and be able to analyse the situation more clearly. Although you may be journalling some deep emotions, seeing them in black and white can let you look at them more as an observer rather than a participant.

It doesn't matter how regularly you write in your journal as long as you have something to reach for when you feel the need to gather your thoughts. Calming thoughts should come much quicker with practice and consistent journalling.

Like a therapy session, if you are releasing your emotions out onto a page, they are no longer seething away inside you, and once out, they will diminish in size.

3. Make sure you laugh

Laughter is balm for the soul. It lifts your emotions, your defences are down, and the load seems lighter. Laughter helps you to find an equilibrium in your mind and soul.

Don't take everything so seriously! This is the biggest barrier to laughter. When you laugh, do it properly. Do things that make you laugh, meet friends, spend time with your children or pets, watch a comedy, as these will lift the darkness of stress.

4. Take a moment away from everything

Take a break. This will help you to pause and gather your thoughts. If you get the chance and don't need to carry out any urgent analysis or information gathering, have a moment of peace. Proper rest requires a total break from all activities that may need some sort of thought, regardless of how innocuous you think these may be.

This break includes any daily chores or duties, in particular. Just relax, breathe and enjoy the moment.

Get some fresh air. Sit outside and breathe in. Watch the world go by. These small moments of calm will help you to focus later when you go back to work as the rest will do you good.

5. Don't spend too much time watching media

Mindlessly watching the media, just because it's there, is a very negative pastime. Doing this can subliminally influence your thoughts and opinions and create beliefs and biases. This can affect decisions you may need to make later, with data unconsciously absorbed weighing you in a certain direction.

If you can concentrate more on where your attention is focused, and the information you are accessing, you can determine whether this is of benefit to your life and wellbeing.

6. Spend more time being creative

Creativity is a wonderful thing. It helps your imagination to run free and expand. It increases curiosity and problem solving. There are so many ways of embracing creativity, whether it be through cooking a new recipe, painting, singing or dancing.

Letting your imagination run wild can bring back some of the wonderment and innocence of youth. Once you have chosen an activity that can let you reconnect with your inner child, explore it to its limits.

7. Make time for exercise

Regardless of the type of exercise you have chosen, make sure you are moving and working up a sweat. Exercise releases endorphins. There are other benefits of course, such as helping you to stay healthy and avoid illnesses, keep your energy levels up, maintain a healthy weight, and make sure that you are keeping positive. A regular exercise regime helps with your sleep patterns, your focus levels and makes you feel good.

Make sure that you choose a form of exercise that will continue to keep you interested, motivated and challenged. There are so many options, from running, yoga or dancing. The method that suits you will help you enjoy a healthier lifestyle and will help to improve your mental health fitness levels.

8. Know what your priorities are

Identify your priorities in life by listing what's important to you – your goals, relationships and motivations. This list can then be put in order of importance, which can be used to allocate your time spent on each. This can help you to improve your sense of wellbeing as you can spend time on the things that you love.

Once you have figured out your priorities, you can analyse the barriers to them. What is stopping you from spending quality time doing the things that you love? This can be used to perhaps change your situation to match what needs to be done.

9. Be kind to others

By helping others, you help yourself. Don't be afraid to step in if a situation doesn't feel right. Letting a dubious situation carry on can have just as much effect on you, even if you are not directly involved.

Although it may not make sense, by giving, you may sometimes receive. To receive love, you must give it, and this applies to many things in life, both personal or financial.

Showing kindness is something you should do every day.

This can be something as simple as a smile. This small but positive action can cheer someone up, but can give you a sense of compassion and positivity. This will bring down any barrier you may have between your conscious mind and the unconscious part that is naturally compassionate.

10. Don't hold on

Worrying gets you nowhere. When worrying feelings appear and increase over time, it's important to let it go. This is because worrying uses up all of our energies and distracts us from the important things in life.

Like our homes, we sometimes need to spring clean! Negative thoughts can take over our minds, filling them with fear, pressure and stress. We can become overwhelmed with peer judgements and the weight of expectations. The best way to deal with this is to cut out negative feelings and replace them with positive ones. If you can manage this, you will notice a dramatic and positive difference in your life.

Keep Your Life Balanced

Surprises are a part of life that we have no control over. How we manage them is what counts. By dealing effectively with each thing that life throws at us we can maintain an equilibrium that satisfies our needs. We can't see the future, but we can view unpredictability, not as something to dread, but as an opportunity to explore new things.

Teach Your Brain to Remain Focused

As an entrepreneur, a large workload is part of the job description. With so many things pushing and pulling you in all directions it can be hard to remain focused. However, even in a chaotic work environment it is possible to train yourself to stay focussed. Knowing what you can handle will help you to use your strengths and increase productivity.

The rise of technology in the workplace has had incredible benefits, but also negative side effects. One of these is distraction. David Rock, writer of the popular book, 'Your Brain at Work', and the co-founder of the 'NeuroLeadership Institute', explains that becoming distracted is an indication that a change has occurred. He considers a distraction as a warning sign that we must focus on the issue as, until we do, we cannot determine whether it is a possible danger or not. This reflex is not something that we can easily suppress as it is an involuntary action.

The ability to multitask is both necessary and damaging. David Rock has claimed that multitasking is actually detrimental to a person's IQ, that it actually works against a person's intelligence levels. Multitasking increases our chances of making mistakes as we are trying to do too many things at once. Small hints are given, like simple spelling mistakes, that should remind us to concentrate on one thing at a time.

Unfortunately, when we multitask, we feel good. We can do it all! As David Rock explains, when we multitask, we feel as if we are really using our brains. It's not realistic to completely eliminate distractions, but it should be possible to put aside 20 minutes a day to focus on just one task at a time. If you can achieve this, you will find it makes a difference to the way that you concentrate and get work done.

There are three top tips that you can use to help you to increase both your productivity and your ability to focus at work:

1. Start with work that is more creative

Many people begin their day's work with the easy tasks, with the intent of moving on to the more challenging ones later. This is a guaranteed way to burn through your energies. As we go through the day, our energy levels are depleted, which can dramatically decrease our powers of focusing. As per David Rock, every decision that we make throughout the day makes the brain more tired.

A simple solution to this is to start with the hard jobs. Those tasks that need a greater amount of creativity or a higher level of concentration, should be tackled first. This leaves the simpler jobs for later – deleting old messages, shredding, etc.

2. Set up a schedule that works and manage your time properly

A study carried out by David Rock discovered that we only concentrate effectively for about six hours per week. This result was discovered through extensive research with thousands of participants and was based on their habits. This would give you an idea of how important it is to analyse your day and to make sure that you are using your time in the most effective manner.

Further research indicated that the most productive environment was not the working one but time away from the office; late at night or first thing in the morning. To best use your focus, it's a good idea to identify the time where you are least destructive and most creative. This is the time to schedule your most difficult tasks.

3. Treat Your Mind as a Muscle When Training

The more often you allow yourself to multitask, the more adjusted your mind will become to working on more than one thing. Distractions become more of a probability, and your mind will start to forget how to remain focused and will instead anticipate distractions. David Rock explained this as our brain becoming tuned into unfocusing automatically.

Focusing needs to be worked at. You need to take the time to eliminate distractions and just do one job at a time. It's best to start off with short periods of concentration and build them up to longer periods. When you feel your mind wandering, try and pull it back to finish your job. David Rock likened this to muscle training, explaining that the longer you train the longer your mind will be able to focus. As with exercise, the longer you work out, the fitter you will become.

RISK MANAGEMENT

Risk management is one of the key components of successful trading. You may question the reason for this, but simply put it is this. The aim of trading is to make a profit and if you do not put a risk management process in place you leave yourself open to heavy losses.

A risk management plan can explain potential risks, so by recognising them you might be able to avoid them and, in turn, avoid losses.

Unfortunately, risk management is not frequently practised among traders. Due to the rapid nature of the trading environment, traders usually get caught up in the urgency of trading and don't stop to consider their situation. Instead of devising their trading strategy and sticking to it, they disregard caution. Cross their fingers and hit 'trade'.

This is not trading: this is gambling and is the reality of your activities if you do not make use of risk management activities.

Gamblers do not have a long-term strategy, they are after the quick and easy option and expect to hit the jackpot. They have no skill, don't prepare or research and put no fail-safes in place. This is not the proper way to trade.

Risk management will provide other benefits. Statisticians are more successful than gamblers because, although both can lose money, the former can control their losses better. Controlling your losses is at the heart of risk management. You have a better chance of making money if you can control your losses.

Trading in the Forex market is a skilled game of numbers in which every aspect needs to be taken into account. Taking a casino as an example: casinos have approximately % over a gambler, but this is what determines who wins and who loses. We want to be on the side that wins! If you take a statistician into consideration, in comparison to a gambler, they will have a much better chance of being profitable.

How Much Do You Need In Your Account To Start Forex Trading?

There is a saying that says, "it takes money to make money" and this is especially true in the case of the Forex market. It's a basic requirement of trading that you need capital (trading capital) to trade. What's not so obvious is how much. This is not a straightforward answer as it depends on the trader and the type of venture they propose to set up. Before we look at that, however, there are a few things that you need to take into account.

Special Tools

The second most important thing that you need to think about are the tools that you will need to use. Charting software and accessible news broadcasts are vital. There are quite a few charting programmes, some are excellent. Our recommendation is TradingView, an online source that provides live quotes and free charts.

You may be a full-time, professional trader with access to instant news feeds. These are a vital tool in your kit but can be exorbitantly priced. If you are lucky, you may have these bills (up to several thousand per month) paid for by your Forex broker. Or, if you are one of those who does not have access, that fraction of a second that you miss out on can make or break your trade.

Money to Trade

Your final ingredient is capital. This is necessary to commence trading. You absolutely need money, capital or funds to begin trading. There are some Forex brokers who propose account deposits with a minimum of $25. Although it sounds great, don't take the bait! This is a certain path to failure. You have to expect to make losses; it's an integral part of trading. Losses in itself will not put you under. What will hit you, however, is not enough funds to cover these losses.

If you are looking for definitive answers to the question "How much capital should I have in my account before I enter the fray?" and if you are a consistent Forex trader who makes strong use of risk management procedures, then between £10k to £100k is your range. This amount can be further narrowed down by asking yourself if this will be your only source of income. This will determine your figure more accurately.

It is common business knowledge that the reason for the failure of the majority of businesses is undercapitalisation. This is applicable to the Forex market too. This means that if you can't afford to lose money it might be advisable to take a break, save some money, and re-enter the market when you are able to. This could be discouraging but waiting until you are ready is the much wiser option in the long-term.

Drawdown and Maximum Drawdown

We have looked at how important risk management is for successful trading, but now let's look at it from another angle and see what might happen if you didn't apply it. Have a look at the following example:

You have £100,000 capital, but you lose £50,000. How much have you lost?

Very simply, 50% of your capital. This is known as a drawdown, which is the amount you have lost following a series of unsuccessful trades. A maximum drawdown measures the difference between the highest peak and subsequent trough.

Traders usually express this in terms of a percentage of their account.

Losing Streak

Traders constantly search for an advantage. Their systems and processes are specifically designed for this very purpose. Let's say you have a trading system that earns 70% profit, that might appear to be a good percentage.

However, that does not mean that out of every 100 trades, 70 of them will be successful. There may be no guarantee in what order the successes and losses will occur. You may lose the first 30 and earn large for the next 70.

Seventy percent sounds like good odds but if you lost the first 30 trades could you afford to carry on or would your account be cleared out?

This shows the reasoning behind risk management and why it is so important. The type of system you employ is not important; what matters is that you have a strategy. However, it is important to actually use your strategy. As a Forex trader you need to understand that you will sometimes experience losses and even a losing streak. This is part of the job. The important issue is whether you can recover from these losses.

If you have devised a profitable, tried and tested strategy then it's advised to maintain it even throughout your losing streak. Don't try to change or abandon it in the middle of your streak. You need to take into account the precise market conditions that you are working in and to make sure that your strategy is best suited to these.

A losing streak can be disheartening but don't lose faith in your strategy because of it. It can be tempting to think that your strategy is the reason for your losses and try something else, but if you do this you will never have consistent success. Forex traders are successful when they apply favourable probability to their strategies. Each strategy has its own edge, and as long as this remains you should continue to trade.

You will never see Casino Heads come down to interrupt blackjack players because the house is losing money. They know that luck will change and their profits will eventually return. They are confident in their slight edge and know they just need to wait for it to come back.

Think of yourself as a Casino Head: take confidence from your statistical advantage and let the statistics take care of themselves.

Even lesser experienced Forex traders can follow these guidelines and follow this train of thought. It's a good idea to establish a trial account to test out your strategy. If it works, great, trust it. Give it some time to settle and when you are ready you will know if this is the strategy for you.

Trade Risk Management Table

2% risk Table

10 % risk table.

2% Risk Strategy: In the first table, as you continue to place trades with a 2% risk, you can observe how your account balance decreases alongside the risk amount after each trade.

2% RISK ON EACH TRADE	TOTAL ACCOUNT	2% RISK
Trade #	Account Balance	Risk Amount
1	$20,000	$400
2	$19,600	$392
3	$19,208	$384
4	$18,824	$376
5	$18,447	$369
6	$18,078	$362
7	$17,717	$354
8	$17,363	$347
9	$17,015	$340
10	$16,675	$333
11	$16,341	$327
12	$16,015	$320
13	$15,694	$314
14	$15,380	$308
15	$15,073	$301
16	$14,771	$295
17	$14,476	$290
18	$14,186	$284
19	$13,903	$278

10% RISK ON EACH TRADE	TOTAL ACCOUNT	10% RISK
Trade #	Account Balance	Risk Amount
1	$20,000	$2,000
2	$18,000	$1,800
3	$16,200	$1,620
4	$14,580	$1,458
5	$13,122	$1,312
6	$11,810	$1,181
7	$10,629	$1,063
8	$9,566	$957
9	$8,609	$861
10	$7,748	$775
11	$6,974	$697
12	$6,276	$628
13	$5,649	$565
14	$5,084	$508
15	$4,575	$458
16	$4,118	$412
17	$3,706	$371
18	$3,335	$334
19	$3,002	$300

10% Risk Strategy: The second table outlines the 10% risk per trade, demonstrating how quickly your account value can be affected when taking higher risks.

Both tables illustrate the importance of managing your trading risks effectively and understanding how losses can accumulate over time. By being aware of your risk exposure in each trade, you can make more informed decisions in your trading journey.

Risking 2% vs. 10% Per Trade

The chart shows the large difference between risking 2% of your account and risking 10% of your account on a single trade. Let's assume that you had just had 19 losses consecutively. At 10%, that would have brought down your account from $20,000 to only $3,002, which is a devastating 85% of your account. It would be difficult to recover from this. Your luck would have to dramatically turn in order for you to be able to continue trading.

If you had risked 2% you would have a very different picture. At 2%, 19 consecutive losses would have left you with $13, 903, leaving you with a 30% loss of income. It's still a loss but one that you could recoup from.

In fairness, losing 19 trades in a row would be a worst-case scenario and was done for illustration purposes. However, the chart shows what would happen if you lost more than five consecutive trades and the still significant difference between 2% and 10%.

At 2%, you would still have $18,447 left, but if you risked 10% you would only have $13,122. You would be better off if you had lost all trades at 2%.

The chart and examples are designed to show you the importance of risk management and of devising your own system to refer to. This will allow you to continue trading even after a drawdown, as you will still have money left in your account.

To lose 85% of your account is catastrophic but it happens more often than you might think. Eager traders who jump into trading without the proper preparation and adherence to their risk management plan are the usual culprits. To put this into perspective; if you lost 85%, you would need to earn 566% just to break even. This shows the importance of risk management and why it is so necessary for Forex traders.

How Can I Recover What I have Lost and Break Even?

Prior to looking at this, look at the table below that calculates the amount needed to break even, contingent on the percentage of your loss of capital.

LOSS OF CAPITAL	% REQUIRED TO GET BACK TO BREAKEVEN
10%	11%
20%	25%
30%	43%
40%	67%
50%	100%
60%	150%
70%	233%
80%	400%
90%	900%

Obviously, the more you lose, the more you need to make back to recover from this and break even once again. This may only seem small initially, but once you get to 30% it doubles and triples and by the time you get to 90% you need to earn 900% to break even.

The main thing to take from this is the importance of your risk management strategy, it protects you from events like these happening to you and shows you how necessary it is to adhere to your 2% trading limit.

Hopefully, you have realised the importance of only investing a small percentage of your account per trade by now. Our aim is to show you the main Forex trading mistakes and by explaining them to you, you can avoid them. If you can learn how to prevent drawdown in your account, you will be able to continue when you do actually lose. Try to remember that you are the Casino, not a gambler.

Reward-to-Risk Ratio

A very common question asked by traders is 'when is the best time to trade?' The optimum time to commence trading is when you can be reasonably assured that you will make back three times more than what is being risked.

LOSS	WIN
$1,000	
	$3,000
$1,000	
	$3,000
$1,000	
	$3,000
$1,000	
	$3,000
$1,000	
	$3,000
$5,000	$15,000

This is known as the 3:1 reward-to-risk ratio and is the best method to use to increase your chances of profit. The table below demonstrates how it works.

The table shows that even if only 50% of your trades are successful, you would still profit by $10,000. Remember, though, that in order for this ratio to be effective, you need to maintain a lower percentage rate. If you do this, you will increase your chances of success.

You may think that if you use a higher reward-to-risk ratio that you will increase your chance of profits. Higher percentages earn higher profits! Not so. Check out the following example and see how greater reward-to-risk ratios joined with higher rates will work against you.

You are a scalper who wants to risk 3 pips, but if you use the 3:1 reward to risk ratio you would need to get 9 pips. However, you need to pay the spread, so you are already off to a bad start. The spread is the difference between the buying rate and selling rate.

Next, your broker gives you a spread of 2 pips in the Euro/US dollar rate, so you must acquire 11 pips. This gives you a 4:1 reward to risk ratio, which is not ideal. With this you need to consider that the exchange rate between Euros and dollars could move up and down at any time and you might be instantly shut out if this happens. If you wanted to reduce the amount of the trade bought or sold, also known as a position size, then you should broaden your stop of the reward-to-risk to a ratio better suited to you.

Let's say that you decided to increase the number of pips that you wanted to trade to 50. This means that you would need to earn 153 pips. Because you have altered the position size to work more to your benefit, you have brought the reward-to-risk ratio closer to 3:1.

These are better chances.

It may seem that the guidelines are straightforward, but the reality is that they are more flexible. They can be adapted reliant on the situation, the time frame, and the trading environment, as well as the entry and exit points. Trading environments are changeable and it's best to concentrate on the environment that you are actually active in. Similar to a coach's game plan that depends on the opposition team, it is of benefit to you to know what strategy will best suit the trading environment you find yourself in.

A long-term position trader may feel confident with a reward to risk ratio as high as 10:1, while a scalper may only be comfortable at a 0.7:1.

Risk Management Review

We have covered the reasoning behind using a sound risk management strategy for Forex trading, and although it may seem to be a lot of information, the following are the main points:

- You are the Casino head, not a gambler.
- Think of a Casino as a rich statistician.

- You need money to make money. You need to take into account how much money you can comfortably afford to trade. This is different for each trader and depends on their trading methods.
- Drawdowns will happen; it's an integral part of the process and happens to everyone.
- Set a cap of 2%. It's safer.
- The more you lose, the harder it will be to recover your account amount.

It is vital to remember to only risk a small percentage of your account per trade. Even if you feel you are on a good streak you cannot guarantee it. Your only guarantee is to protect yourself and to trade cleverly or risk heavy losses. Traders need to be able to recover from obstacles, but to be in the business long-term you need to be able to last through losing periods. You need to minimise the drawdowns on your account to survive as a large drawdown could clear you out.

Remember that the less risk you take, the less your maximum drawdown will be. The heavier your losses, the harder it will be to break even, never mind make a profit. If you cannot break even, you may not be able to continue to trade. This is why you need to adhere to the 2% limit on your account. There are of course exceptions to this rule, as it can depend on how often you actually trade, but this is a broad guideline. The smaller you can go, the better.

The greater the currency trades, the less amount of risk you will want to take.

Market volatility is something that must be taken into account when trading in the Forex markets. This can be changed in an instant, by world events, news bulletins or a change in capital. To avoid catastrophe, you need to have entrance and exit strategies formulated.

Regardless of whether you choose to exit on a weakness, strength, or set up a stop and limit approach, always have a plan in place.

Entrance strategies are the same. There are different plans of action available to you but the one you choose will depend on how volatile the market is.

Rules to trade by

1. Limit yourself to between 2-4%.
2. Oversee your trades.
3. To safeguard your profits, move your stop loss.
4. Don't chase your entry point.
5. Even if the market is against you, don't ever lower your stop loss.

FOREX GLOSSARY

A

ACCRUAL
The distribution of premiums and discounts on forward exchange transactions that directly refer to deposit swap (interest arbitrage) deals, for the extent of each deal.

ADJUSTMENT
Authorised modification as a result of changes occurring in either the internal economic policies to amend an inequality in payment, or in the official currency rate.

AGGRESSIVE
Confident trading or price action behaviour.

ANALYST

An experienced trading professional with proficiency in the assessment of investments and can put together buy, sell and hold advice for clients.

APPRECIATION

This is when a product increases in price due to market demand.

ARBITRAGE

Buying and selling a product at the same time to benefit from minute price differences between markets.

ASIAN CENTRAL BANKS

These are the central banks or financial agencies of Asian countries. These have grown in strength over the past few years due to the intensification of their activities in major currencies as they administer increased stores of foreign currency reserves occurring as a result of trade surpluses. They have considerable market interest and influence over short-term currency directions.

ASIAN SESSION

23:00 – 08:00 GMT.

ASK (OFFER) PRICE

This is the value the market puts on a product. Prices are cited two-way as Bid/Ask. Another name for the Ask price is the Offer.

The FX trading Ask price is the price at which a trader can buy the base currency, shown to the left in a currency pair. For example, in the quote USD/CHF 1.4527/32, the base currency is USD, and the Ask price is 1.4532. This means that you can purchase one US dollar for 1.4532 Swiss francs.

In CFD trading, however, the Ask price also represents the price the trader can buy a product for. An example of this is: in the quote for UK OIL 111.13/111.16, the product quoted is UK OIL and the Ask price is £111.16 for one unit of the underlying market.*

AT BEST
This is the optimum price advised to a dealer to buy or sell at during a particular period.

AT OR BETTER
An instruction given to a dealer to buy or sell at a specific price or better. The advice given to a dealer to buy or sell at a particular price or better.

AUS 200
The Australian Securities Exchange (ASX 200), which is a directory of the top 200 companies (by market capitalisation) listed on the Australian stock exchange.

AUSSIE
Jargon expression for the AUD/USD (Australian Dollar/US Dollar) pair. Also "Oz" or "Ozzie".

B

BALANCE OF TRADE

The worth of a country's exports, less its imports.

BAR CHART

A variety of charts comprising four important points: the high and low prices, which form the vertical bar; the opening price, which is denoted with a horizontal line to the left of the bar; and the closing price, which is indicated by a horizontal line to the right of the bar.

BARRIER LEVEL

A price of great significance incorporated into the composition of a Barrier Option. When a Barrier Level price is obtained, the specific Barrier Option terms call for a sequence of actions to happen.

BARRIER OPTION

Those option structures that place great significance on specific price trading. Examples include: knock-in, knock-out, no touch and double-no-touch-DNT. With a no-touch barrier, a large, specified pay-out is given to the buyer of the option by the seller if the strike price is not 'touched' before expiry. This provides motivation for the option seller to push prices through the strike level, and provides a motivation for the option buyer to preserve the strike level.

BASE CURRENCY

This is the first currency denoted in a currency pair. It is an indication of the value of the base currency expressed against the second currency. An example of this is if the USD/CHF (US Dollar/Swiss Franc) rate equals 1.6215, then one USD is worth CHF 1.6215. The US dollar is usually deemed to be the base currency for quotes in the Forex market. This means that quotes are stated as a unit of $1 USD per the other currency quoted in the pair. The main exclusions to this rule are the British pound, the euro and the Australian dollar.

BASE RATE

In any given country, this is the lending rate issued by the central bank.

BASING

This is a chart pattern used in technical analysis. It displays information that describes when demand and supply of a product are nearly the same. The result of this is a narrow trading range and the amalgamation of support and resistance levels.

BASIS POINT

A unit to measure the least amount of change in a product's price.

BEARISH/BEAR MARKET

This is an indication of a negative price direction, one that prefers a weakening market. For example, "We are bearish EUR/USD" means that we think the euro will weaken against the dollar. Bears traders anticipate that prices will fall and might hold short positions.

BID/ASK SPREAD

This is the difference between the bid and the ask (offer) price.

BID PRICE

This is the price at which the market agrees to buy a product. The price is stated two-way as Bid/Ask. In FX trading, the Bid is the price that a trader can sell the base currency, shown to the left in a currency pair. For example, in the quote USD/CHF 1.4527/32, the base currency is USD, and the Bid price is 1.4527, so you can sell one US Dollar for 1.4527 Swiss francs. In CFD trading, the Bid is also the price at which a trader can sell the product. For example, in the quote for UK OIL 111.13/111.16, the Bid price is £111.13 for one unit of the underlying market.*

BIG FIGURE

This is in reference to the first three digits in a currency quote, for example, 117 USD/JPY or 1.26 in EUR/USD. If a price changes by 1.5 big figures, this means that it has moved 150 pips.

BIS

This stands for The Bank for International Settlements and it is headquartered in Basel, Switzerland. It is the central bank over all other central banks and its function is to act as the market arbitrator between national central banks and the market. As central banks have boosted their currency reserve management, the BIS has increased its activities. If the BIS buys or sells at a level, this is generally done for a central bank and so the amounts can be huge. The BIS is responsible for helping markets to avoid mistaking buying or selling interest for official government involvement.

BLACK BOX
These are traders who are methodical, model based or technical.

BLOW OFF
The positive counterpart to surrender. What happens when shorts give up and cover any remaining short positions.

BOC
Bank of Canada, the central bank of Canada.

BOE
Bank of England, the central bank of the UK.

BOJ
Bank of Japan, the central bank of Japan.

BOLLINGER BANDS
A trading tool used by technical analysts. This is a band that is plotted along two typical deviations on both sides of a simple moving average. This can often be a sign of support and resistance levels.

BOND

This is a debt issued for a specific time period.

BOOK

A book, in trading terms, is a synopsis of a trader's, or desk, complete positions.

BRITISH RETAIL CONSORTIUM (BRC) SHOP PRICE INDEX

This is a UK measure of the rate of inflation among several surveyed retailers. This index only takes account of price changes in goods bought in retail stores.

BROKER

A person or company that performs as an arbitrator between buyers and sellers, bringing them together for a fee or commission. A dealer, on the other hand, pledges capital and commits to one side of a position. This is done with the intent of earning profits through a spread, by closing out the position in a following trade with a different group.

BUCK

This has two meanings: slang for one million units of a dollar-based currency pair; or for the US dollar in general.

BULLISH/BULL MARKET

This would indicate a market growing in strength with increasing prices. For example, "We are bullish EUR/USD" means that we expect that the euro will strengthen against the dollar.

BULLS traders anticipate that prices will increase and hold long positions.

BUNDESBANK
Germany's central bank.

BUY
This means to take a long position on a product.

BUY DIPS
This is where a trader tries to buy 20-30-pip/point pullbacks during an intra-day trend.

C

CABLE
This is the GBP/USD (Great British Pound/US Dollar) pair, so called because the rate was originally transmitted to the US via a transatlantic cable. This began in the mid-1800s, when the GBP was the currency of international trade.

CAD
The Canadian dollar, also known as Loonie or Funds.

CALL OPTION
This is a currency trade that makes the most of an interest rate disparity that exists between the two countries. A trader will carry this out by selling a currency with a low rate of interest and buying a

currency with a high rate of interest. The trader will earn the interest difference between the two countries, while this trade is ongoing.

CANADIAN IVEY PURCHASING MANAGERS (CIPM) INDEX

This is a monthly measure of Canadian business attitudes, released by the Richard Ivey Business School.

CANDLESTICK CHART

This is a trading chart that shows the opening and closing price, and trading range, for the day. If the open price is higher than the close price, the rectangle between the open and close price is coloured. If the close price is higher than the open price, that section of the chart is not coloured.

CAPITULATION

The stage towards the end point of an extreme trend when traders with losing positions exit those positions. This is usually a sign that a reversal is imminent.

CARRY TRADE

The carry trade is a trading strategy that involves investors borrowing in a currency with low interest rates and investing in a currency that pays high rates. The classic example of this is NZD/JPY (New Zealand Dollar/Japanese Yen), which has long been a famous carry trade. NZD is the high yielder and JPY is the low yielder. Traders looking to take advantage of this interest rate differential would buy NZD and sell JPY or be long NZD/

JPY. When NZD/JPY begins to downtrend for a long period of time, usually due to a change in interest rates, the carry trade is said to be unwinding

CASH MARKET

A derivatives contract is based on the cash market, which is a market in the actual underlying markets.

CASH PRICE

The real-time price of a product. If you want to buy something now, this will be the price you will pay.

CBS

Acronym for central banks.

CENTRAL BANK

A governmental or semi-state organisation that supervises its country's financial policies and institutions. Examples are the Federal Reserve in the US, and the Bundesbank in Germany.

CFDS*

This stands for Contract for Difference (or CFD) and is a type of derivative that gives exposure to the change in value of an underlying asset (such as an index or equity). It helps traders to control their capital (by trading theoretical amounts much greater than the money in their account) and has all the benefits of trading securities, without actually owning the product. An example is if you buy a CFD at $10 and then sell it at $11, you will receive the $1 difference. However, if you went short on the trade and sold at $10 before buying back at $11, you would pay the $1 difference.

CHARTIST

A type of trader who makes extensive use of charts and graphs and analyses historical information to identify trends and forecast future movements. Also known as a technical trader.

CHOPPY

Short-term price moves with partial follow-through that aren't beneficial to aggressive trading.

CLEARED FUNDS

Accessible funds used to settle a trade.

CLEARING

Settling a trade.

CLOSED POSITION

Exposure to a no longer existing financial contract. For example, a currency. A position can be closed by placing an equal and opposite deal to offset the open position. A closed position is considered squared.

CLOSING

A method of stopping (closing) a live trade by completing a trade that is exactly opposing the open trade.

CLOSING PRICE

A product is traded at this price to close a position. It can also mean the price of the final transaction of a day trading session.

COLLATERAL

As an asset used to obtain a loan, or something used as an assurance of performance.

COMMISSION

A fee charged for the buying or selling of a product.

COMMODITY CURRENCIES

Countries with exports mainly consisting of natural resources have currencies known as commodity currencies. Some of these countries are Canada, Australia, Russia and New Zealand.

COMPONENTS

These are the dollar pairs that the crosses consist of. For example, EUR/USD + USD/JPY are the components of EUR/JPY. Selling the cross through the components is in reference to selling the dollar pairs in rotation to make a cross position.

COMPX

Acronym for NASDAQ Composite Index.

CONFIRMATION

Written contract signed by the participants of a transaction, containing the terms of that transaction.

CONSOLIDATION

A period of time where range-bound activity occurs, following a long price move.

CONSTRUCTION SPENDING

This is a record of the monthly amount of money spent on new construction, released by the US Department of Commerce's Census Bureau.

CONTAGION

Where an economic crisis spreads through various markets.

CONTRACT

This is the standard unit in Forex trading.

CONTRACT NOTE

Some form of proof sent with a description of the precise details of a trade.

CONTRACT SIZE

The notional number of shares in one CFD.

CONTROLLED RISK

Controlled risk refers to a trading position that has a limited or defined level of risk, allowing you to manage potential losses more effectively. This concept is particularly essential in forex trading and other financial markets, where price volatility can lead to significant fluctuations in asset values.

What is Controlled Risk?

A controlled risk position is typically established through the use of risk management tools, the most notable of which is a Guaranteed Stop. A Guaranteed Stop is a special type of stop-loss order that ensures your position will close at the predetermined price level, regardless of market conditions. This means that if the market moves against you, your trade will automatically exit at the guaranteed stop level, thereby protecting your capital from larger, unexpected losses.

CONVERGENCE OF MAS
A technical statement explaining the moving averages of different stages moving towards each other, which usually predicts a price consolidation.

CORPORATE ACTION
Some type of corporate event that can alter the equity structure and, sometimes, the share price of a stock. Examples of these events are acquisitions, dividends, mergers, splits and spin offs.

CORPORATES
Market organisations that engage in hedging or financial management activities. These organisations are usually hardier in terms of price sensitivity than speculative funds and they have long-term interests. This makes these organisations less valuable to short-term traders.

COUNTER CURRENCY

The second listed currency in a currency pair.

COUNTERPARTY

One of the contributors to a monetary transaction.

COUNTRY RISK

Any risks involved with cross-border transactions, for example, legal and political conditions.

CPI

Acronym for Consumer Price Index, which measures inflation.

CRATER

The market is in a position to sell-off hard.

CROSS

A currency pair, not including the US dollar.

CROWN CURRENCIES

These are the currencies of the Commonwealth countries: CAD (Canadian Dollar), Aussie (Australian Dollar), Sterling (British Pound) and Kiwi (New Zealand Dollar).

CTAS

Acronym for commodity trading advisors who are speculative traders with pursuits similar to that of short-term hedge funds; usually means Chicago-based or futures-oriented traders.

CURRENCY
Any type of money licensed by a government or central bank and used as legal tender and a foundation for trade.

CURRENCY PAIR
The two currencies in a foreign exchange rate, an example being EUR/USD (Euro/US Dollar).

CURRENCY RISK
The chance of a negative change in exchange rates.

CURRENCY SYMBOLS
A three-letter representation of a certain currency, for example, USD (US Dollar).They provide a standardised way to identify and represent different currencies, facilitating clear communication and accurate transactions within the global financial markets.

What are Currency Symbols?

Currency symbols are typically composed of three letters, creating a unique identifier for each currency. This three-letter code is known as a currency code and is standardised by the International Organization for Standardization (ISO) under the ISO 4217 standard. The first two letters of the currency code generally represent the country or geographical area, while the third letter denotes the specific currency.

USD: US Dollar
EUR: Euro
GBP: British Pound Sterling
JPY: Japanese Yen
AUD: Australian Dollar
CAD: Canadian Dollar
CHF: Swiss Franc
NZD: New Zealand Dollar

CURRENT ACCOUNT

The total of the sum of the balance of trade (exports minus imports of goods and services), net factor income (such as interest and dividends) and net transfer payments (such as foreign aid). The balance of trade is usually the key element to the current account.

D

DAY TRADER

These are those speculators who take positions in commodities but then liquidate those positions before the close of the same trading day.

DAY TRADING

Opening and closing a trade on a product in one trading day.

DEAL
This is a trade carried out at the current market price. It is considered a live trade, in contrast to an order.

DEALER
the term "dealer" refers to a company or individual that acts as a principal or counterparty to a transaction. Dealers play a crucial role in the financial markets by facilitating trades and maintaining liquidity. They are involved directly in buying and selling assets, such as currency pairs in the forex market, with the intention of earning a profit through the spread – the difference between the buying price (ask) and selling price (bid).

Role of Dealers in Trading

When you engage in retail trading, you may interact with a dealer when executing trades. Dealers take on the risk associated with holding positions; they decide on one aspect of a position, such as the price at which they are willing to buy or sell an asset. For instance, if you wish to buy euros against US dollars, you would place a buy order through a dealer who provides the necessary liquidity to execute your trade.

Dealers operate in various markets, including forex, stocks, and commodities, and are essential for ensuring that transactions can occur smoothly and efficiently. They make money by marking up the spread, which is the profit made from trading activities. This means that as you execute a trade, the dealer is simultaneously managing their positions and seeking opportunities to close out those positions profitably with other counterparties.

Distinction Between Dealers and Brokers

It's important to distinguish between dealers and brokers, as they serve different roles in the trading ecosystem. While both engage in buying and selling financial instruments, a broker acts as an intermediary between buyers and sellers rather than taking on the risk of holding positions themselves. Brokers facilitate trades by matching clients' orders to buy and sell, charging a fee or commission for their services.

For example, when you place an order through a forex broker, the broker may route your trade to a dealer. In this situation, the broker earns a commission for executing your order, while the dealer earns the spread by taking the other side of the transaction. Understanding this distinction can help you choose the right trading structure based on your trading needs and preferences.

Example of a Dealer in Action

Consider you are trading the GBP/USD currency pair and decide to buy £1,000 at an exchange rate of 1.3000. When you place this order, the dealer provides you with the price quote. Let's assume the dealer quotes you a buy price of 1.3000 and a sell price of 1.2980. The difference of 20 pips represents the dealer's spread. If the market moves, and you decide to sell your position shortly after at the quoted sell price of 1.2980, the dealer records a profit from the spread.

In this scenario, you are able to execute your trade quickly, thanks to the dealer providing liquidity. The prompt execution allows you to react to market conditions effectively, highlighting the dealer's essential role in enabling your trading activities.

DEALING SPREAD

In a contract, this is the difference between the selling and the buying price.

DEFEND A LEVEL

A trader, or group of traders will do this to stop a product trading at a specific price, or within a price zone, because they have an interest in doing so. For example, a barrier option.

DEFICIT

Payments or trade with a negative balance.

DELISTING

To de-list a stock from the exchange it is trading on.

DELIVERY

A type of trade where each side makes and takes delivery of the traded product.

DELTA

The ratio calculated between a product's price change and the price change of its underlying market.

DEPARTMENT OF COMMUNITIES AND LOCAL GOVERNMENT (DCLG) UK HOUSE PRICES

A monthly survey, released by the DCLG, carried out on a large sample of all finalised house sales. It shows all of the price trends in the UK housing market.

DEPRECIATION

This is the reduction in value that an asset experiences over time.

DERIVATIVE

A type of financial contract with a value determined by the value of an underlying asset. Examples of the most common underlying assets for derivative contracts are indices, equities, commodities and currencies.

DEVALUATION

This is when a pegged currency is let weaken or devalue depending on official behaviour. This is the opposite of a revaluation.

DISCOUNT RATE

This is the interest rate charged by the Federal Reserve Bank to an eligible depository institution when it lends funds.

DIVERGENCE

This describes an event, in technical analysis, where price and momentum are going in opposite directions, for example, prices increasing while momentum falls. Divergence is thought to be either positive (bullish) or negative (bearish), but the two types of divergence indicate huge changes in price direction. Positive/bullish divergence happens when a security price hits a new low while the momentum indicator starts to increase. Negative/bearish divergence occurs when the security price hits a new high, but the indicator does not instead move lower. Divergences often happen in extended price moves and usually settle with the price reversing direction to follow the momentum indicator.

DIVERGENCE OF MAS

A technical opinion that usually predicts a price trend, by explaining moving averages of different periods moving away from each other.

DIVIDEND

A company's earnings or profits are divided proportionately among its shareholders. Otherwise known as a value per share.

DJIA OR DOW

Short form of the Dow Jones Industrial Average or US30.

DOVE

This expression means a data or policy opinion that prefers an easing in monetary policy or lower interest rates. It's the opposite of hawkish.

DOWNTREND

Price action consists of lower lows and lower highs.

DXY$Y

Stands for the US Dollar Index.

E

ECB

The European Central Bank, the central bank for the countries within the Eurozone.

ECONOMIC INDICATOR

A statistic released by the government that details the present economic growth and security. The main indicators are employment rates, Gross Domestic Product (GDP), inflation and retail sales.

END OF DAY ORDER (EOD)

An order that says to buy or sell at a certain price that stays open until the trading day closes, which is usually 5pm/17:00 New York time.

EST/EDT
Acronym for Eastern Standard Time/Eastern Daylight time. Or the timezone of New York, US.

ESTX50
The Euronext 50 Index.

EURO
The currency of the Eurozone.

EUROPEAN MONETARY UNION (EMU)
A collective name for those policies that synchronise the economic and fiscal policies for the EU Member States.

EUROPEAN SESSION
07:00 – 16:00 (London).

EUROZONE LABOUR COST INDEX
A measure of the yearly rate of inflation for pay and benefits paid to national workers. Is considered the main driver of inflation in general.

EUROZONE ORGANIZATION FOR ECONOMIC CO-OPERATION AND DEVELOPMENT (OECD) LEADING INDICATOR
A monthly index published by the OECD. This calculates the overall economic health of the Eurozone by amalgamating ten main indicators, including average weekly hours, new orders,

consumer expectations, housing permits, stock prices and interest rate spreads.

EX-DIVIDEND

A buyer buys a share but waives the right to get the next dividend, which is given to the seller instead.

EXPIRY DATE/PRICE

The exact moment of expiry for an option. The two most common examples of this are 10:00 am ET (also referred to as 10:00 NY time or NY cut) and 3:00 pm Tokyo time (also referred to as 15:00 Tokyo or Tokyo cut). There is usually increased activity leading up to these times as option hedges unwind in the spot market.

EXPORTERS

Organisations who sell their goods abroad. This makes them sellers of foreign currency and buyers of their domestic currency. Examples of exporters are huge Japanese companies such as Sony and Toyota, who are sellers of USD/JPY and exchange dollars earned from commercial sales abroad.

EXTENDED

A market considered to have travelled too far, too fast.

F

FACTORY ORDERS

This is the dollar level of new orders for durable and non-durable goods. It is a more detailed report than the durable goods report, issued earlier in the month.

FED

The Federal Reserve Bank, the central bank of the United States, otherwise known as the FOMC (Federal Open Market Committee), the policy-setting committee for the Federal Reserve.

FED OFFICIALS

Members of the Board of Governors of the Federal Reserve or regional Federal Reserve Bank Presidents.

FIGURE/THE FIGURE

This is the price quotation of '00' in a price such as 00-03 (1.2600-03), read as 'figure-three.' If someone sells at 1.2600, traders would say 'the figure was given', or 'the figure was hit'.

FILL

A fully executed order is said to be 'filled'.

FILL OR KILL

An order has to be filled, but if it is not, it will be expunged (killed).

FIRST IN FIRST OUT (FIFO)

A currency pair has all its positions liquidated in the order in which they were first opened.

FIX

There are five fixed times during the Forex trading day when huge sums of currency must be bought or sold to fulfil commercial customers' orders. These times are connected to periods of market instability. These times are as follows (all NY times):

5:00 am - Frankfurt
6:00 am - London
10:00am - HMHCO (World Market House Company)
11:00am - HMHCO (World Market House Company) - more important
8:20am - IMM
8:15am - ECB

FLAT OR FLAT READING

Economic data that is unchanged from the previous period's data.

FLAT/SQUARE

Trading slang for a position that has been totally reversed. For example, you bought $500,000 and then sold $500,000, which created a neutral (flat) position.

FOLLOW-THROUGH

Renewed interest in trading following a directional break of a specific price level. The absence of follow-through usually means a directional move will not be continued and indeed may reverse.

FOMC

Federal Open Market Committee, this is the policy-setting committee of the US Federal Reserve.

FOMC MINUTES

These are the detailed records of the FOMC policy-setting meetings and are published three weeks after each meeting. They provide perception into the FOMC's discussions and negotiations, and can incite substantial market responses.

FOREIGN EXCHANGE/FOREX/FX

The act of buying one currency at the same time as selling another. This global market is known as the Forex or FX market.

FORWARD

A foreign exchange contract detailing the agreed exchange rate to sell at an agreed future date. This is based on the interest rate differential between the two currencies in negotiation.

FORWARD POINTS

These are the pips added to or taken away from the present exchange rate so as to determine a forward price.

FRA40

This is an index of the French stock exchange listing the top 40 companies (by market capitalisation). It can also be called the CAC40.

FTSE 100

The UK 100 index.

FUNDAMENTAL ANALYSIS

An analysis of all of the available information on a potentially tradeable product to identify its potential and hopefully the direction of its price. Non-measurable and personal assessments, as well as quantifiable measurements, are usually made in fundamental analysis.

FUNDS

Active hedge funds in the Forex market. Can also refer to the USD/CAD (US Dollar/Canadian Dollar) pair.

FUTURE

A contract between two participants to complete a transaction at an agreed date in the future at a price agreed in the present.

FUTURES CONTRACT

A contract to trade a good or service at an agreed price, a detailed quantity grade, at a date in the future. The main difference between a Future and a Forward is that Futures are usually traded over an exchange (Exchange-Traded Contacts - ETC), while Forwards are considered Over The Counter

(OTC) contracts. An OTC is any contract that is NOT traded on an exchange.

G

G7

Group of 7 Nations – United States, Japan, Germany, United Kingdom, France, Italy and Canada.

G8

Group of 8 – G7 nations plus Russia.

GAP/GAPPING

A rapid market movement where prices miss several levels with no trades taking place. This usually happens after economic data or news bulletins.

GEARING (ALSO KNOWN AS LEVERAGE)

Gearing is where a trade of a notional value occurs that is larger than the capital amount a trader needs to hold in their trading account. It is stated as a percentage or a fraction.

GER30

Or the DAX, is an index of the top 30 companies (by market capitalization) listed on the German stock exchange.

GIVEN

This is a selling interest, or a bid being hit.

GIVING IT UP

This is when a technical level gives in to a hard-fought fight.

GMT (GREENWICH MEAN TIME)

This is the main time zone used in the Forex Market. It does not change during the year, for example during daylight savings/ summer time.

GOING LONG

Buying a stock, commodity or currency for investment or speculation purposes, with the anticipation that the price will increase.

GOING SHORT

Where a seller sells a currency or product that they don't own, with the anticipation that the price will drop.

GOD (GOD'S RELATIONSHIP)

It is well known that gold moves in a direction opposite to the US dollar. In other words, the long-term correlation coefficient is mostly negative, but shorter-term correlations are less dependable.

GOLD CERTIFICATE

A certificate of ownership used in place of the physical gold, which makes it easier for gold investors to purchase and sell the commodity instead of having to transfer and store the actual gold.

GOLD CONTRACT

This is the standard unit for trading gold. One contract is equal to 10 troy ounces.

GOOD FOR DAY

An order that, if it is not filled, will elapse at the end of the day.

GOOD 'TIL CANCELLED ORDER (GTC)

An order to buy or sell at a stated price that will stay open until filled or the client revokes the order.

GOOD 'TILL DATE

An order that will elapse on a date of your choosing, if it is not previously filled.

GREENBACK

Slang name for the US dollar.

GROSS DOMESTIC PRODUCT (GDP)

The worth of a country's entire output, income or expenditure created inside its physical borders.

GROSS NATIONAL PRODUCT

The total sum of GDP in addition to income earned from investment or work abroad.

GUARANTEED ORDER

A type of order that shields a trader from gaps in the market. It is a guarantee to fill your order at the asking price.

GUARANTEED STOP

A type of stop-loss order pledged to close your position at a level determined by you if the market moves to, or past, that point. It is guaranteed even if there is a market gap.

GUNNING/GUNNED

This is where traders try to set off known stops or technical levels in the market.

H

HANDLE

All of the 100 pips in the Forex market that begin with 000.

HAWK/HAWKISH

Hawkish is when the financial policy makers in a country consider that increased interest rates are necessary to keep inflation under control or to calm fast economic growth, or both.

HEDGE

A position, or amalgamation of positions, that protects your primary position from risk.

HIT THE BID

To sell at the current market bid.

HK50/HKHI
The Hong Kong Hang Seng index.

I

ILLIQUID
When only a small volume is traded in the market. This lack of liquidity often makes for fluctuating market circumstances.

IMM
The International Monetary Market; based in Chicago, this is a currency futures market, which comes under the Chicago Mercantile Exchange.

IMM FUTURES
A conventional futures contract established on major currencies against the US dollar. IMMI futures are traded on the Chicago Mercantile Exchange floor.

IMM SESSION
This is from 8:00am - 3:00pm New York time.

INDU
Abbreviation for the Dow Jones Industrial Average.

INDUSTRIAL PRODUCTION

Determines the aggregate output value generated by manufacturers, mines and utilities. This information is able to respond quickly to expansions and contractions of the business cycle and can give an indication of employment and personal income data.

INFLATION

An economic situation where consumer goods prices increase, which depletes purchasing power.

INITIAL MARGIN REQUIREMENT

The primary payment needed to enter into a position.

INTERBANK RATES

This is the foreign exchange rates quoted between large international banks.

INTEREST

Money charged on a loan or repayment as a payment for that transaction.

INTERVENTION

Intercession carried out by a central bank to influence the value of its currency by entering the market. Concerted intervention means the actions of several central banks to regulate exchange rates.

INTRODUCING BROKER
A trader or organisation who introduces accounts to brokers for a payment.

INX
Symbol for S&P 500 index.

IPO
An Initial Public Offering (IPO) is a critical milestone for any private company, marking its transition into the public domain by offering shares of its stock to the general public for the first time. This process allows a private company to raise capital from public investors, which can then be used for various purposes such as expansion, paying off debt, or funding new projects. For retail traders, understanding IPOs is essential, as they provide unique investment opportunities and insights into market dynamics.

What Happens During an IPO?

When a company decides to go public, it hires investment banks to act as underwriters. These banks assist the company in determining the appropriate price per share and the number of shares to be issued. Once the offering is set, the shares are made available on a stock exchange, allowing investors to buy them for the first time.

PRE-IPO SHARES

Pre-IPO shares refer to stock that is issued by a private company prior to its Initial Public Offering (IPO). These shares are typically offered to select investors, such as institutional investors, venture capitalists, private equity firms, and sometimes high-net-worth individuals, before the company goes public and sells shares to the general public on a stock exchange. For retail traders, gaining an understanding of pre-IPO shares can provide valuable insights into investment opportunities and the dynamics of capital raising for companies.

Characteristics of Pre-IPO Shares

Investment Opportunity: Investing in pre-IPO shares offers an opportunity to acquire equity in a promising company before its shares become available to the public. For retail investors who can access these shares, it may lead to significant potential returns if the company performs well following its public debut.

Restricted Access: Generally, pre-IPO shares are not widely available to the average retail trader. Access is often limited to accredited investors or those involved in private equity funding. This exclusivity can make it difficult for everyday investors to purchase these shares unless they are part of investment groups or syndicates that focus on pre-IPO opportunities.

Valuation Considerations: Pre-IPO shares are valued based on factors such as the company's financial performance, growth prospects, and the amount of capital it aims to raise through the IPO.

ISM MANUFACTURING INDEX

An index that measures the status of the manufacturing sector in the US by questioning executives on future production prospects, new orders, inventories, employment and deliveries. On the index, any value over 50 usually means an expansion, and values below 50 mean a contraction.

ISM NON-MANUFACTURING

This index questions service sector companies for their viewpoint. It includes the other 80% of the US economy not included in the ISM Manufacturing Report. Again, on this index, any value over 50 usually means an expansion and values below 50 mean a contraction.

J

JAPANESE ECONOMY WATCHERS SURVEY

This survey gauges the sentiment of businesses in the services industry, for example, waiters, drivers and beauticians. Values over 50 usually mean increased sentiment.

JAPANESE MACHINE TOOL ORDERS

This is a measure of the entire value of new orders consigned with the manufacturers of machine tools. These orders are a gauge of the demand for organisations that manufacture machines, which is a strong indicator of the prospects of industrial production. Strong data usually indicates improvements in manufacturing and that the economy is expanding.

JPN225
The NIKKEI index.

K

KEEP THE POWDER DRY
To minimise your trades because of extreme trading environments. If there are choppy or extremely narrow markets, it's better to stay out of the way until a better chance comes around.

KIWI
Slang name for NZD/USD (New Zealand Dollar/US Dollar).

KNOCK-INS
This is an option strategy that needs the core product to trade at a particular price prior to a previously purchased option becoming active. It is used to minimise the premium costs of the core option and can activate hedging pursuits as soon as an option is activated.

KNOCK-OUTS
This is an option that invalidates an option purchased previously if the core product trades at a certain level. Then a knock-out level is traded, the core option no longer exists and any hedging might have to be unwound.

L

LAST DEALING DAY

A particular product's final available day to trade.

LAST DEALING TIME

The final time you can trade a particular product.

LEADING INDICATORS

Statistical data that are believed to forecast prospective economic movement.

LEVEL

A specific price or price zone that is important from a technical point of view or centred on reported orders/option interest.

LEVERAGE

Another term for margin. From your available capital, this is the percentage or fractional increase you can trade from. This allows traders to trade speculative values much greater than the capital that they actually have. An example of this is leverage of 100:1 denotes that you can trade a notional value 100 times greater than the capital in your trading account.*

LEVERAGED NAMES

Among the hedge-fund community this refers to short-term traders.

LIABILITY

Debt, financial responsibility or prospective losses.

LIBOR

London Interbank Offered Rate, used as a base rate for international lending.

LIMITS/LIMIT ORDER

An order that tries to buy at a level lower than the current market rate or sell at a higher level than the current market rate. A limit order creates boundaries on the highest price to be paid or the lowest price to be received. For example, if the current price of USD/JPY is 117.00/05, then a limit order to buy USD would be at a price below the current market, e.g. 116.50.

LIQUID MARKET

A market with enough buyers and sellers for the price to move smoothly.

LIQUIDATION

Closing a current position by the completion of an offsetting transaction.

LONDON SESSION

08:00 – 17:00 (London).

LONG POSITION

Essentially, a long position refers to a situation in which you purchase a currency pair with the expectation that its price will increase. When you take out a long position, you are buying the base currency while simultaneously selling the quote currency. This strategy allows you to profit from upward price movements in the market.

What is a Long Position?

A long position is taken when you believe that the value of a currency will rise in the future. For example, let's consider a common currency pair like the EUR/USD. When you open a long position on EUR/USD, you are buying euros (the base currency) and selling US dollars (the quote currency).

If the current exchange rate is 1.1000, it means that 1 euro is equivalent to 1.10 US dollars. Should you decide to purchase this currency pair, you would be hoping that the price will increase. For instance, if the exchange rate rises to 1.1200, your long position would now be profitable, as you can sell the euros you bought at a higher rate than what you initially paid.

Profit Potential

The value of your long position increases when the market prices of the currency pair rise. For example, if you bought 1,000 euros at the rate of 1.1000, your initial investment in US dollars would be $1,100 (1,000 euros x 1.1000). If the price subsequently rises to 1.1200, and you decide to close your position by selling the euros, you would receive $1,120 (1,000 euros x 1.1200). The profit from this transaction would be $20 ($1,120 - $1,100), illustrating how you can benefit from a positive price movement in a long position.

LONGS
Traders who have purchased a product.

LOONIE
Trading slang for the Canadian dollar or the USD/CAD (US Dollar/Canadian Dollar) currency pair.

LOT
A unit of measurement to calculate the amount of a deal. The value of the deal always matches an integer number of lots.

M

MACRO
The longest of the term traders who determine their trade decisions on basic analysis. The holding period of a macro trade can be as short as six months and as long as several years.

MANUFACTURING PRODUCTION
This is a measurement of the total production of the manufacturing section of the Industrial Production data. This data is limited to the 13 sub-sectors directly related to manufacturing. Manufacturing is responsible for about 80% of total Industrial Production.

MARGIN CALL
An application from a dealer or broker for extra finances or other security for a position that has moved against the customer.

MARKET MAKER
A dealer who can offer both ask and bid prices and is willing to create a two-sided market for any financial product.

MARKET ORDER
An order to sell or buy at the present price.

MARKET-TO-MARKET
This is a method of reassessing all open positions due to current market prices. Any updated values control margin needs.

MATURITY
The date when a financial product is settled or expires.

MEDLEY REPORT
Reports issued by Medley Global Advisors, a market consultancy group that have close ties with central banks and government agencies worldwide. These reports can often influence the currency market as they claim to have confidential information from policy makers. The level of accuracy of these reports has been variable in the long-term, but in the short-term they can still affect the market.

MODELS
The same as a black box. Systems that routinely buy and sell are founded on technical analysis or other quantitative algorithms.

MOM

Acronym for month-over-month. These are the alterations in a data series in comparison to the previous month's level.

MOMENTUM

A sequence of technical investigations (e.g. RSI, MACD, Stochastics, Momentum) that evaluate the degree of price changes.

MOMENTUM PLAYERS

Traders that are affiliated with an intra-day trend that aims to grab 50-100 pips.

N

NAS100

The NASDAQ 100 index.

NET POSITION

The total amount of currency bought or sold that has not been counteracted by any converse trades.

NEW YORK SESSION

8:00am – 5:00pm (New York time).

NO TOUCH

This is an option that remunerates a set sum to the holder if the market does not touch the predetermined Barrier Level.

NYA.X
The NYSE Composite index.

O

OFFER/ASK PRICE
This is the value the market puts on a product. Prices are cited two-way as Bid/Offer. Another name for the Offer price is the Ask.

The FX trading Ask price is the price at which a trader can buy the base currency, shown to the left in a currency pair. For example, in the quote USD/CHF 1.4527/32, the base currency is USD, and the Ask price is 1.4532. This means that you can purchase one US dollar for 1.4532 Swiss francs.

In CFD trading however, the Ask price also represents the price the trader can buy a product for. An example of this is: in the quote for UK OIL 111.13/111.16, the product quoted is UK OIL and the Ask price is £111.16 for one unit of the underlying market.*

OFFERED
When a market is described as trading offers this means that a pair is causing intense selling interest or offers.

OFFSETTING TRANSACTION
A trade that revokes or offsets some or all of the market risk contained in an open position.

ON TOP

Trying to sell at the current market order price.

ONE CANCELS THE OTHER ORDER (OCO)

A description for two orders where if one order is executed, the other order is consequentially cancelled.

ONE TOUCH

This is an option that remunerates a set sum to the holder if the market touches the predetermined Barrier Level.

OPEN ORDER

An order that will be carried out when a market reaches its selected price. Usually connected to good 'til cancelled orders.

OPEN POSITION

An open trade with an equivalent unrealised P&L, that has not been counterbalanced by an equal and opposite trade.

OPTION

A derivative that offers the right, but not a compulsion, to purchase or sell a product at a certain price prior to an agreed date.

ORDER

A directive to complete a trade.

ORDER BOOK

A procedure for identifying the market depth of traders who will buy and sell at prices over and above the best on offer.

OVER THE COUNTER (OTC)

Transactions that are not carried out through an exchange.

OVERNIGHT POSITION

A trade that stays open until the following business day.

P

PAID

This is the offer aspect of the market trading.

PAIR

The Forex method of quoting by matching one currency against another.

PANELLED

A substantial round of selling.

PARABOLIC

This describes a market that moves a long distance over a short time. It often moves in an increasingly fast pattern that looks like one half of a parabola. These parabolic moves can be both up or down.

PARTIAL FILL

When an order has been only partially completed.

PATIENT

Holding off on trading for an anticipated level or news bulletins to reach the market, prior to entering a position.

PERSONAL INCOME

This is an individual's overall annual gross earnings comprising salary, business dealings and all of their investments. Personal income is the basis for personal spending and this makes up two-thirds of GDP in most major economies.

PIPS

Any foreign currency's smallest unit of price. Pips actually refer to the digits added to or subtracted from the fourth decimal place, for example, 0.0001.

POLITICAL RISK

Government policy adjustments that may subject an investor to negative consequences on their position.

PORTFOLIO

A compilation of investments possessed by a person or group.

POSITION
The total net holdings of a specified product.

PREMIUM
The total sum by which the forward or futures price surpasses the spot price.

PRICE TRANSPARENCY
Those quotes that every market member can access equally.

PROFIT
The figure calculated between the cost price and the sale prices, specifically when the sale price is greater than the cost price.

PULLBACK
The propensity of a trending market to review a portion of the gains, prior to continuing in the same direction.

PURCHASING MANAGERS INDEX (PMI)
An economic index used to determine the performance of manufacturing companies in a country.

PURCHASING MANAGERS INDEX SERVICES (FRANCE, GERMANY, EUROZONE, UK)
Determines the prospects of service sector purchasing managers. These managers are questioned on a variety of topics, such as

employment, production, new orders, supplier deliveries and inventories. Results above 50 usually show expansion, while results below 50 implies economic contraction.

PUT OPTION
This is where an owner has the permission to sell at a determined price but does not have to.

Q

QUANTITATIVE EASING
Quantitative Easing (QE) is a monetary policy tool used by central banks to stimulate the economy, particularly in times of economic downturn or when traditional monetary policy measures, such as lowering interest rates, become less effective. For retail traders, understanding QE is crucial, as it can significantly influence market conditions, asset prices, and trading strategies.

What is Quantitative Easing?

Quantitative Easing involves a central bank purchasing financial assets, such as government bonds and mortgage-backed securities, from the market. By doing so, the central bank injects liquidity into the economy, increasing the money supply. The goal of QE is to lower interest rates and increase lending and investment, thereby boosting economic activity.

When a central bank initiates QE, it effectively increases the reserves of commercial banks, encouraging them to lend more. This increased lending can spur consumer spending and business investment, leading to higher economic growth. In essence, QE aims to stimulate the economy when it is sluggish by encouraging borrowing and spending.

QUARTERLY CFDS
A specific category of future with every three month (once per quarter) expiry dates.*

QUOTE
A suggestive market price, typically only used for information.

R

RALLY
This is when a price upturns following a period of decline.

RANGE
This is when a price is trading between a specified high and low, moving between the two boundaries but not breaking out from them.

RATE
Stating the price of one currency in terms of another. This is normally used for dealing reasons.

RBA

The Reserve Bank of Australia, the central bank of Australia.

RBNZ

The Reserve Bank of New Zealand, the central bank of New Zealand.

REAL MONEY

These are the traders who deal in larger sized accounts. They include pension funds, asset managers, insurance companies, etc. They are seen as signs of major long-term market interest, in contrast to shorter-term, intra-day investors.

REALISED PROFIT/LOSS

This is the total sum of money that you have gained or lost once a position has been closed.

RESISTANCE LEVEL

A price that can function as a limit. The opposite of support.

RETAIL INVESTOR

This is a solo investor who trades with personal money/accounts instead of trading for an institution.

RETAIL SALES

This is a gauge of the monthly retail sales of the total goods and services sold by retailers based on a selection of various categories and sizes. This information gives an idea of the status of consumer spending behaviour, which in turn is a main factor in the growth of all of the major economies.

REVALUATION
This is when a pegged currency is encouraged to strengthen or increase due to official interventions. This is the opposite of devaluation.

RIGHTS ISSUE
A type of commercial action that gives shareholders the right to buy more stock. These are usually issued by corporations to raise additional capital.

RISK
To face the possibility of indeterminate change, usually used in a negative manner in association with adverse change.

RISK MANAGEMENT
To use financial analysis and trading techniques to control or reduce your chances of facing a multiple of detrimental risks.

ROLLOVER
This is an activity that involves the concurrent closing of an open position for today's value date and the opening of the same position for the next day's value date at a price indicating the difference in the interest rate between the two currencies.

The guideline in the spot Forex market is that trades need to be settled within two business days. An example of this would be where a trader sells 100,000 Euros on Tuesday, then he must deliver 100,000 Euros on Thursday, unless the position is rolled over. As part of its normal workings, the Forex market automatically rolls over all open positions at the end of the day (5:00 pm New York time) to the next settlement date.

ROUND TRIP

This is a trade that has been opened and then closed by an equal but opposite transaction.

RUNNING PROFIT/LOSS

A guide to the state of your open positions. In other words, unattained money that you would earn or lose if you closed all of your open positions at that time.

RUT

Acronym for Russell 2000 index.

S

SEC

The Securities and Exchange Commission.

SECTOR

A collection of securities that trade in a comparable industry.

SELL

Deciding on a short position in the hope that the market will go down.

SETTLEMENT

How a trade is input into the records. This is a register of the parties to a deal. Settling a currency trade does not have to involve a physical transfer of one currency for another.

SHGA.X

Acronym for the Shanghai A index.

SHORT-COVERING

Traders who went short following a decline now begin to buy back.

SHORT POSITION

An investment position that gains from a reduction in market price. The position is described as short when the base currency in the pair is sold.

SHORT SQUEEZE

A state where traders position heavily on the short side, but a market catalyst makes them cover (buy) quickly, which creates a dramatic price increase.

SHORTS

This is a trader who has sold, or shorted a product, or one who is bearish on the market.

SIDELINES, SIT ON HANDS

This describes those traders who stay out of the market because of a lack of obvious direction or choppy or unclear market directions.

SIMPLE MOVING AVERAGE SMA

A simple average of a pre-delineated amount of price bars. An example of this is where a 50-period daily chart SMA is the average closing price of the previous 50 daily closing bars. You can apply any time interval for this.

SLIPPAGE

In a situation where market conditions influence the price, slippage is the difference between the price asked for and the price received.

SLIPPERY

This is an expression used for when the market seems like it's about to move rapidly in any direction.

SLOPPY

Irregular trading situations without any perceivable trends and/or follow through.

SNB

Swiss National Bank, the central bank of Switzerland.

SOVEREIGN NAMES

These are the central banks trading in the spot market.

SPOT MARKET
A market where products are traded for their market price and immediately change hands.

SPOT PRICE
The market price right now. Settlement of spot transactions has a guide of two business days for completion.

SPOT TRADE
A product is bought or sold for delivery straight away (and not a date in the future). Spot contracts are usually settled electronically.

SPREAD
The difference between the bid price and offer price.

SPX500
The S&P index.

SQUARE
There is an equilibrium between purchase and sales, so the dealer can have no open position.

STERLING
A name for the British pound or the GBP/USD (Great British Pound/US Dollar) currency pair.

STOCK EXCHANGE
A financial market where securities are traded.

STOCK INDEX

The total price of an amalgamation of stocks, stated against a base number, to calculate how the group of companies is performing compared to in the past.

STOP ENTRY ORDER

An order placed to buy above the current price, or to sell below the current price. This type of order is good for when you consider that the market is going in a certain direction and you have an entry price goal.

STOP-LOSS HUNTING

When a market seems to be reaching for a certain level that is believed to be heavy with stops. If stops are triggered, then the price will often jump through the level as a flood of stop-loss orders are triggered.

STOP LOSS ORDER

This is a vital risk management tool where an order is placed to sell below the current price (to close a long position), or to buy above the current price (to close a short position). If you set your stop loss order against open positions, you can minimise your risk downside if the market moves against you. It's important to note that stop orders are not a guarantee of your execution price – a stop order is initiated as soon as the stop price is reached and will be carried out at the next available price.

STOP ORDER

This is an order given to buy or sell as soon as a predetermined price is reached. When this occurs, the stop order becomes a market order and is completed at the best obtainable price. Remember that stop orders can be influenced by market gaps and slippage and may not necessarily be carried out at the stop level if the market does not trade at this price. A stop order will be filled at the next available price as soon as the stop level has been reached. Even if you place contingent orders, you might not restrain your losses.

STOPS BUILDING

This refers to a backlog, or build up, of stop-loss orders; the accrual of stop-loss orders to buy above the market in an up move, or to sell below the market in a down move.

STRIKE PRICE

The price specified where the option holder can buy or sell the product.

SUPPORT

A price floor for past or future price movements.

SUPPORT LEVELS

A technical analysis method that specifies a certain price ceiling and floor where a given exchange rate will spontaneously correct itself. This is the opposite of resistance.

SUSPENDED TRADING

A brief pause in the trading of a product.

SWAP

A currency swap is where a sale and purchase of an equal amount of a specified currency is simultaneously completed at a forward exchange rate.

SWISSIE

A jargon expression for the Swiss franc or the USD/CHF (US Dollar/Swiss Franc) currency pair.

T

TAKEOVER

Taking control of a company through the purchase of its stock.

TECHNICAL ANALYSIS

The analysis of charts containing past price patterns to find indications as to any possible directions of future price movements.

TECHNICIANS/TECHS

These are traders who form their trading decisions and positions on the analysis of charts and other technical data.

TEN

(10) YR US government-issued debt, which is repayable in ten years. For example, a US 10-year note.

THIN

A non-liquid, slippery or choppy market conditions, or a low volume market that creates unpredictable trading conditions.

THIRTY

(30) YR UK government-issued debt which is repayable in 30 years. For example, a UK 30-year gilt.

TICK (SIZE)

The minimum up or down change in price.

TIME TO MATURITY

The remaining time is a contract until it expires.

TOKYO SESSION

09:00 – 18:00 (Tokyo).

TOMORROW NEXT (TOM/NEXT)

The buying and selling of a currency at the same time for delivery the next day.

T/P

This refers to “take profit” and means limit orders that try to sell above the level that was purchased, or to buy back beneath the level that was sold.

TRADE BALANCE

Calculates the difference in value between imported and exported goods and services. Countries such as Japan, with trade surfers usually see their currencies increase in value, while countries such as the US, with trade deficits (their imports outnumber their exports) usually see their currencies weaken.

TRADE SIZE

In a contract or lot, the volume of product.

TRADING BID

When a pair acts strongly and moves higher, bids continue to enter the market, increasing the prices even more.

TRADING HALT

Deferring trading, but not a suspension from trading.

TRADING HEAVY

A market that should move lower. This describes an offered market that doesn't rally, in spite of buying efforts.

TRADING OFFERED

When a pair is weak and moves lower and bids to sell continue to enter the market.

TRADING RANGE

This is the range between the highest and lowest stock price, normally stated referring to a time period, for example, a 52-week trading range.

TRAILING STOP

This permits a trade to keep gaining in value when a market price is moving in a favourable direction, but instantly closes the trade if the market price decides to move in an unfavourable direction by a predetermined direction. The placing of contingent orders may not reduce your losses.

TRANSACTION COST

The cost of buying or selling a financial product.

TRANSACTION DATE

The date on which a trade occurs.

TREND

This is a movement in price that creates a net change in value. An uptrend can be recognised by higher highs and higher lows. A downtrend can be recognised by lower highs and lower lows.

TURNOVER

The total financial value or volume of all transactions carried out during a specific time period.

TWO-WAY PRICE

This is when a bid and offer rate are both quoted for a Forex deal.

TYO10

The CBOE 10-Year Treasury Yield Index.

U

UGLY

Market conditions that are challenging and demanding and also merciless and fast.

UK AVERAGE EARNINGS INCLUDING BONUS/ EXCLUDING BONUS

This is a measure of the average remuneration including/ excluding bonuses paid to employees. It is calculated quarter-on-quarter (QoQ) from the previous year.

UK CLAIMANT COUNT RATE

This is data collected to count the total number of people claiming unemployment benefits. This figure is usually lower than the unemployment figure because not all unemployed people are entitled to benefits.

UK HBOS HOUSE PRICE INDEX

This index is a measure of the comparative level of house prices in the UK. It shows trends in the UK real estate market and the importance of these for the UK's economic prospects. It is the longest monthly data series of all UK housing indices, and is printed by the largest UK mortgage lender, Halifax/Bank of Scotland.

UK JOBLESS CLAIMS CHANGE

A measure of variations in the amount of people claiming unemployment benefits compared to the previous month.

UK MANUAL UNIT WAGE LOSS

This calculates any changes in overall labour costs used in the manufacture of one unit of output.

UK OIL*

Brent Crude Oil.

UK PRODUCERS PRICE INDEX INPUT

This calculates the inflation rate faced by manufacturers when buying goods and services. This is important information and is closely monitored because it can indicate consumer inflation.

UK PRODUCERS PRICE INDEX OUTPUT

This index calculates the inflation rate faced by manufacturers when selling goods and services.

UK100

The FTSE 100 index. The UK100, commonly known as the FTSE 100 index, is one of the premier stock market indices in the United Kingdom. It is comprised of the 100 largest companies listed on the London Stock Exchange (LSE) by market capitalisation and is considered a benchmark for measuring the performance of the UK stock market. As a retail trader, understanding the UK100 is essential, as it provides valuable insights into the overall health of the UK economy and market trends.

Composition of the FTSE 100 Index

The FTSE 100 index includes a diverse array of companies spanning various sectors including finance, healthcare, consumer goods, and energy. Prominent firms such as BP, HSBC, and Unilever are part of this index, making it a significant representation of the UK corporate landscape. Because the index is weighted by market capitalisation, larger companies have a more substantial influence on the index's movements.

UNDERLYING
This is the traded market where a product's price originates from.

UNEMPLOYMENT RATE
The unemployment rate is a key economic indicator that measures the percentage of the labour force that is unemployed and actively seeking employment. In retail trading, particularly in the context of forex and stock trading, the unemployment rate serves as a vital gauge of economic health and can significantly impact market sentiment, influencing trading decisions.

Importance of the Unemployment Rate

For you as a retail trader, the unemployment rate offers valuable insights into the overall economy. A high unemployment rate often signals economic distress, indicating that many individuals are without work, which can lead to reduced consumer spending and lower overall economic growth. Conversely, a low unemployment rate suggests a robust economy, typically associated with increased consumer confidence and spending power.

These dynamics make the unemployment rate a critical factor in understanding potential market movements. For instance, when unemployment is low, you may anticipate positive market performance, as companies are likely to benefit from a consumer base with greater disposable income. Conversely, rising unemployment can lead to bearish sentiment in the market, as fears of economic contraction and reduced corporate profits may set in.

UNIVERSITY OF MICHIGAN'S CONSUMER SENTIMENT INDEX

The university surveys 500 US families every month and the resulting report is released twice per month: an initial version mid-month; and the finished version at the end of the month. The questions are based on the attitudes of individuals towards the US economy and the resulting answers on consumer sentiment are seen as an indication of consumer spending.

UNREALIZED GAIN/LOSS

The theoretical gain or loss on open positions valued at current market rates, as determined by the broker in its sole discretion. Unrealized gains/losses become profits/losses when the position is closed. A hypothetical loss or gain made on open positions valued at current market rates. This is decided by the broker. Unrealized gains/losses become profits/losses once the position closes.

UPTICK
An updated price quote that is higher than the previous quote.

UPTICK RULE
A US regulation where a security cannot be sold short unless the previous trade had a lower price than the price that the short sale is sold for.

US OIL
US Oil, often referred to as West Texas Intermediate (WTI), is one of the most widely traded commodities in the world and serves as a benchmark for oil prices globally. It is a grade of crude oil originating from the United States, specifically from oil fields in Texas and surrounding regions. The significance of US Oil extends beyond just fuel; it plays a critical role in the broader economy and financial markets, making it a popular asset for retail traders.

Characteristics of US Oil

In retail trading, US Oil is typically traded as a futures contract on exchanges such as the New York Mercantile Exchange (NYMEX) and is denoted by the ticker symbol CL. One of the key characteristics of US Oil is its relatively low sulphur content, which makes it easier and more economical to refine into various petroleum products, including gasoline and diesel fuel.

WTI Crude Oil.

US PRIME RATE
The interest rate at which US banks will lend to their prime corporate customers. This is the interest rate that US banks use for their main corporate clients.

US30
The Dow Jones index.

The Dow Jones Industrial Average (DJIA), commonly referred to as the Dow Jones index, is one of the most widely recognised stock market indices in the world. It serves as a key indicator of the overall health of the US economy and is often used by retail traders to gauge market performance and make informed trading decisions.

Composition of the Dow Jones Index

The Dow Jones index comprises 30 large and influential publicly traded companies, primarily based in the United States. These companies are leaders in their respective industries and represent a diverse array of sectors, including technology, finance, healthcare, and consumer goods. Since the index is price-weighted, each company's influence on the index is proportional to its stock price; thus, higher-priced stocks have a more significant impact on the index's movement than lower-priced stocks.

Importance of the Dow Jones Index

For you as a retail trader, the Dow Jones index serves multiple purposes. First and foremost, it provides a snapshot of market sentiment and economic conditions. When the index rises, it typically reflects investor confidence and a thriving economy, while a falling index may signal uncertainty or economic challenges. Therefore, monitoring the performance of the Dow can help you make informed decisions about your investment strategies.

V

VALUE DATE
This is the agreed date by which traders or buyers must discharge their debts, i.e. pay their bills. Spot currency transactions normally have a value date of two business days.

VARIATION MARGIN
This is the amount traders need to have in their accounts to ensure that they have the necessary funds to cover any market irregularities.

VIX OR VOLATILITY INDEX
This is an indication of the volatility levels of the market for the next 30 days. It is compiled of data regarding prospective volatility of an extensive span of S&P 500 index options. The VIX is an often -used indicator or market risk and is commonly known as the "investor fear gauge".

VOLATILITY

Describes active markets with plenty of trade opportunities.

W

WEDGE CHART PATTERN

This is a chart configuration that demonstrates a narrowing price range over a period of time. It mainly shows where price highs in an ascending wedge decrease proportionately, or in a descending wedge, price declines are proportionately smaller. Ascending wedges usually end with a downside breakout and descending wedges usually end with upside breakouts.

WHIPSAW

Vernacular expression for a very unpredictable market with a sudden price movement followed by a sudden reversal.

WHOLESALE PRICES

This is a measure of the price changes paid by retailers for completed products. Inflationary pressures are usually seen before headline retail.

WORKING ORDER

This is when a limit order has been called for but hasn't yet been filled.

WSJ

Acronym for The Wall Street Journal.

XXAG/USD
Symbol for Silver Index.

XAU/USD
Symbol for Gold Index.

XAX.X
Symbol for AMEX Composite Index.

Y

YARD
A billion units.

YIELD

The percentage return earned from an investment.

YOY
Acronym for year over year.

YUAN
The main unit of currency in China is the Yuan. The currency where the Yuan is the base unit is called the renminbi.

Z
Dedicated to Lon Chan

www.ingramcontent.com/pod-product-compliance
Lightning Source LLC
Chambersburg PA
CBHW071534200326
41519CB00021BB/6479
9781917329637